APOLOGETICS

APOLOGETICS

A Class Manual in the Philosophy
of the Catholic Religion

By

RIGHT REV. MSGR. PAUL J. GLENN, PH.D., S.T.D.

PRESIDENT OF COLLEGE-SEMINARY OF
ST. CHARLES BORROMEO, COLUMBUS, O.

TAN BOOKS AND PUBLISHERS, INC.
Rockford, Illinois 61105

NIHIL OBSTAT

> *Rt. Rev. Joseph A. Weigand,*
>
> *Censor Deputatus*

IMPRIMATUR

> ✠ *James J. Hartley, D.D.,*
>
> *Bishop of Columbus*

Originally published by
B. Herder Book Co., St. Louis, Missouri

Copyright © 1931 by B. Herder Book Co.

Copyright © 1980 by TAN Books and Publishers, Inc.

Library of Congress Catalog No.: 80-51330

ISBN: 0-89555-157-8

Printed and bound in the United States of America

Sixteenth printing

TAN BOOKS AND PUBLISHERS, INC.
P. O. Box 424
Rockford, Illinois 61105

1980

This little Book on the Sanity of the Catholic Religion is dedicated, with Love abounding, to the fadeless Memory of Two who loved that Religion through long and stainless Years, and were Its ardent Apologists in Word, in Deed, and in all their Lives,

MY FATHER AND MOTHER,

who are now, these many Years, with God in Heaven

PREFACE

At the present moment there is great need for textbooks in Christian Apologetics or Evidences. Perhaps there is even greater need for texts in Christian Polemics. For it does seem that Catholics might at last refuse to deal seriously with the insanities charged against their religion. It does seem that Catholics might now take the active and aggressive stand in the endless argument that goes on about their faith; that they might now, after so many, many weary refutations of absurdities, require proofs from their opponents instead of silly charges, and positive doctrine instead of the vague sentimentalism and tiresome negations that make up the jejune sectarianism of our day. Still, however delightful it would be to charge happily into the part of "the offensive" and turn out a textbook that would serve Catholic students by instructing them in methods of making the enemies of the true faith consider the cheapness and inadequacy of their own resources, it is well to resist the pleasant impulse to do it. For successful Polemics can come only from sound Apologetics. Let the Catholic student learn and love to be a thorough apologist for his religion; let him delight in the scientific knowledge of the reasonableness and necessity of his own true faith. Then, and then only, will he be equipped for positive warfare against falsehood. Then, and then only, will he be able to show the unreason and the unmanliness of irreligion, and to dissipate the fog of sentimentality that passes for religion with many moderns. Let us then have textbooks in Apologetics.

The class manual in Apologetics needed to-day has a somewhat peculiar shape. Two or three generations ago, a text in this subject had mainly to deal with the unique truth of the Catholic religion among many religions, all claiming to be Christian. Among people of our western civilization at least, it was then quite generally admitted that there is a God and that Christ is God-made-Man; Christ's Church was admitted to be the only true Church, and the question that concerned the apologist was—which, among several claimants, is really Christ's Church? To-day, outside the Catholic Church, the existence of God is specially ignored, and the divinity of Christ is generally denied, even by sectarian clergymen. The modern textbook in Apologetics must, therefore, deal more fully than the older texts with the fundamental truths of God's existence and the divinity of Christ. And the modern chapter on the claims of the Catholic Church, as distinct from other Christian bodies, may be made much more brief and direct, for the simple reason that the "other Christian bodies" have largely faded into a vaguely differentiated group with no very positive claims of any kind except the general claim to the right of taking "centre shots at Rome," as a bright little modern book has it.

This textbook was written in a sincere effort to supply what is felt as a distinct need. It tries to present a clear and logical statement of the philosophy, the *reason,* that is back of the Catholic religion. It endeavors to impress upon the student the necessity under which every educated Catholic lies, of being interested in the reasonableness of his religion and of realizing his duty to make non-Catholics interested in it. It tries to offer a course of training that will make Catholic students understand that they have a warfare to conduct, but not a "warring against flesh and blood"; that they are soldiers active for Christ, not to inflict the shame of a defeat, but to share the glory of a victory; that they are militant marchers in a hostile world, not bearing chains to bind, but bringing the inestimable treasure of the truth that makes men free.

May this book serve, then, however feebly, the glorious purpose for which it was composed.

P. J. G.

College of St. Charles Borromeo
Columbus

CONTENTS

BOOK SECOND

RELIGION

BOOK THIRD

CHRIST

BOOK FOURTH

THE CHURCH

INTRODUCTION

1. Name   2. Definition   3. Importance   4. Division

1. NAME

The word *apologetics* is derived from the Greek word *apologeisthai*, which means "to defend oneself." The words *apology* and *apologia* derive from the same source. Thus, the basic meaning of *apology*, *apologia* and *apologetics*, is the same, viz., "self-defence" or "justification of one's position, conduct, or belief." The vulgar meaning of the word *apology*, which makes it synonymous with *excuse*, is excluded from our use of the term. To make an apology, or to present an apologetic is not, therefore, to admit being in the wrong; on the contrary, it is to explain that one is in the right. *Apologetics* means a justification, a vindication, a satisfactory explanation.

2. DEFINITION

Apologetics is the science which explains and justifies the Catholic religion as the true religion.

Apologetics is a *science,* that is to say, it is a body of certainly known facts, set forth in a manner that is systematic, logical, and complete; and it presents the reasons which show these facts to be true and certain.

Apologetics is a *human* science, for it draws its

facts from history and philosophy (i. e., *human*
sources) and develops its proofs by unaided human
reason. Apologetics does not call upon Divine Revelation (as the *divine* science of theology does) for its
fundamental proofs; but it regards the records of
Revelation as historical documents until they have
been proved by reason to be the teachings of the infinite and infallible God.

Apologetics *explains and justifies the Catholic religion as the true religion.* That is to say, Apologetics
shows that the Catholic religion in its essentials, and
in such individual doctrines as may be investigated
by the unaided mind of man, is reasonable, right, and
true; and it shows that the arguments used against
the claims of the Catholic religion are unwarranted,
unreasonable, and fallacious.

3. IMPORTANCE

You may say: "I am a Catholic. I know perfectly
well that my religion is the one true religion. I have
no need of a scientific study to convince me of its
unique truth. I possess the infused gift of faith, and
I realize, moreover, that my religion is thoroughly
reasonable. What care I for the attacks and slurs directed against it by ignorance and prejudice? I need
no Apologetics to show me that such attacks and slurs
are utterly unreasonable and unjust. Therefore, the
study of Apologetics does not appear important to
me."

Your objection misses the point. Apologetics is not meant to convince *you* of the truth of your religion, but to equip you for the task of convincing others. Apologetics is not meant to rationalize your faith; for faith is a divine gift far surpassing mere intellectual conviction. But faith and intellect are gifts of the one God, and between them there is a perfect and beautiful harmony. To discover this harmony, and to indicate it in a scientific manner for the benefit of others, is the opportunity offered you in the study of Apologetics. This opportunity you must embrace. For, as an educated Catholic, you are required to do more than possess your faith in security, and to bear with patience the slights cast upon it by unreason and prejudice; you must be able to banish prejudice from minds that entertain it. Those who misunderstand your religion, and hate it, and speak all manner of evil things against it, are human beings with souls that God wants saved, and He expects you to do your part in saving them. Now, you may do very much for the saving of such souls by disposing them intellectually to receive the divine gift of faith. Apologetics seeks to fit you for this service, and it is, therefore, a very important study—in fact, it is the most important study you could possibly undertake.

Again, although you rightly say that you need no argument or scientific proof to convince you of the truth of your religion, you may be placed in circumstances in which you will find a knowledge of Apologetics a strong bulwark against the weakening or even the loss of your faith. Many Catholic parents, in spite of the clearly defined wishes of the Church, send their sons and daughters to colleges and universities in which little is heard of God or the dignity and destiny of man, and much is made of the pseudo-science which rules all religion out of account. Suppose you are sent to such a school. Professors will smile tolerantly or scoff openly at your religion; your fellows will sneer at your piety; lax and lapsed Catholics on the campus will urge you by example, and probably also by word, to abate the ardent practice of your religion and to conform yourself to the pattern approved by the school. Day after day, week after week, month after month, you will live in an atmosphere of contemptuous opposition to all that you love and revere. You will breathe perforce the contagion of that atmosphere. And what then? Unless you are a thorough apologist for your faith, unless you have a ready and adequate answer for the cleverly worded arguments used against it, you may feel that perhaps, after all, your position is not altogether safe and certain. You may find yourself thinking, "Surely these learned professors cannot be altogether wrong; there must be some grain of truth in what all these others are saying." And thus you will stand in danger of a horrible degradation, namely, of withdrawing your faith from God and reposing it in man. Faith you will have in any case;

man simply *must* have faith. But what an unspeakable thing it is to transfer one's faith from the All-Wise and the Infinitely True to a sneering professor, a picayune and priggish pedagogue. Now, a thorough knowledge of Apologetics is a strong defence against this sort of spiritual putrefaction. You perceive, then, that this study is important—for yourself as well as for others.

Even if the future does not hold out to you the prospect (and the menace) of secular university life, you have still a real need for the study of Apologetics. In the office, in the club, in social contacts with friends and acquaintances, you are sure to find much hatred of your religion, hatred that comes largely of misinformation. There are too many Catholics, even educated Catholics, who meet that hatred with an excuse instead of a true apologetic. Do not swell the ranks of these shrinking and unworthy soldiers of Christ. Realize the importance of Apologetics, and give this science your most earnest study.

Where you fail to encounter hatred against your religion, you will find indifference towards it. You will find people interested in the things they eat, in the garments they wear, in the amusements with which they are diverted, in the matters of business to which they attend, in the journeys they plan to make, in the fortunes they hope to build up, in the careers they aspire to achieve, and in all manner of things that have no value passing this life. Here again is an atmosphere hostile to your religion, an atmosphere that spiritual writers call "the world." Now a true apologist can do much to purify the worldly atmosphere; he can win the attention of worldly minds and make them less worldly; he can gain a respectful hearing when such minds are made to realize that he has sound reasons to offer in defence of his faith, and not mere emotional or sentimental argument. Once more you perceive that Apologetics is a science of supreme importance.

Finally, what science could be more important than that which brings man's noblest faculties to bear upon the most excellent object of study, viz., God and the things of God? What culture is there to compare with the culture of soul which comes of the recognition and appreciation of infinite truth? Is there any true culture possible in minds that regard religion as futile or as a mere agglomeration of tender sentiments? Certainly, there is no cultured Catholic who is not an able and ardent apologist for his faith. Therefore, you dare not call the study of Apologetics unimportant; on the contrary, you must acknowledge it as incomparably the greatest and most important study in your entire programme.

4. DIVISION

The truths that Apologetics establishes are these: That God exists, one, infinite, all-perfect; the creator and conserver of the universe; the ruler of all things. That man is bound to recognize his utter dependence upon God by acknowledging Him and serving Him in the practice of the true religion. That the true religion is that of Our Lord Jesus Christ, who is true God and true Man. That the true religion of Christ is that of the Catholic Church.

These truths indicate the four departments of Apologetics, which may be named as follows: God, Religion, Christ, The Church.

Under these four heads we shall develop our study of Apologetics. The present treatise is accordingly divided into four Books, with Chapters as follows:

BOOK FIRST

GOD

This Book offers rational proofs for the existence of God, and reasons out the truth about His nature and attributes. It then studies the action of God on the world, and shows that God is the creator, conserver, and ruler of the universe. The Book is accordingly divided into three Chapters, as follows:

CHAPTER I

THE EXISTENCE OF GOD

This Chapter offers rational proofs for the existence of God. That God exists we already know by the divine gift of faith, by revelation, by grace, by training, and by our own direct thought upon the realities and requirements of life. We know that God exists, not because something proves it, but because everything proves it; not because a certain syllogism demonstrates it, but because our rational nature absolutely requires it.

When we analyze a few of the proofs that wise men have formulated for the tremendous truth of God's existence, we undertake a task of some delicacy and even danger. We may find ourselves thinking, as the reasoning process of proof is tediously developed, and as argument is marshaled after argument, that there may be room for questioning what requires such an elaborate process of evidence. On the other hand—so variable is the human viewpoint—we may come to think that the arguments here presented are very few, and make but a sorry basis for the intellectual conviction of so grand a truth as that of God's existence. Let us keep our common sense. Let us remember that this elaborate process of evidence is not requisite, but possible, and that our whole purpose is to show that it is possible. We do not need proofs to convince ourselves of the existence of God; we develop them so that reason may attain its highest function, and so that those who demand rational proof of God's existence may be forced to admit that such proof is available. And if the thought strikes us that these arguments are few, let us recognize the obvious fact that our task is like that of men who dig down to find and study some few of the roots of a giant tree. We do not think that these few roots are all that hold the tree in its place, erect in storm and wind; we know that there are a hundred other roots, each with a hundred sturdy radicels, all firmly grounded and secure, which are not the object of our present study. In a word, while the arguments offered are conclusive and incontrovertible, we do not seek to rationalize faith, but merely to record some of the compelling reasons which show that faith is justified by the natural power of the human mind. Meanwhile we hold fast to the divinely given belief which needs no argument, and to the natural conviction of mind which is the result in us of the converging evidence of all the experiences of rational and practical life.

This Chapter presents five proofs for the existence of God. Each proof is studied in a special Article. The Chapter is accordingly divided into five Articles, as follows:

Article 1. The Argument from Cause
Article 2. The Argument from Motion
Article 3. The Argument from Design
Article 4. The Argument from the Moral Order
Article 5. The Argument from History

ARTICLE 1. THE ARGUMENT FROM CAUSE

a) Doctrine of Causality   b) The Argument   c) Discussion of the Argument

a) DOCTRINE OF CAUSALITY

A *cause* is that which contributes in any manner whatever to the production of a thing. The thing produced is called an *effect*. The relation of a cause towards its effect is called *causality*.

The world around us is a tissue of the cause-and-effect relation, i. e., of causality. The movement of the earth and the heavenly bodies is the cause of re-current night and day and of the change of seasons. The laws of Nature are but formulas which express the existence and relations of causes and effects. Plants, brutes, and men live and grow by the causal activity of an inner life-principle and by the supple-mentary causes of light, heat, air, moisture, food, which enable this life-principle to function. Every-where we see causes at work producing effects, and we see effects, in their turn, becoming causes of fur-ther effects. The sun, for example, is the cause of sunlight; sunlight is the cause of sunburn; sunburn is the cause of pain; pain is the cause of sleeplessness, etc.—the example may be extended indefinitely. We need no further example, however, to convince us of these facts: (1) Causality exists in the world. (2) The effect of one cause may become the cause of fur-ther effects. (3) The chains of cause and effect may be crossed and interwoven at innumerable points, so that many causes may converge to produce one ef-fect, and the influence of one cause may be found in various effects.

So obvious is the existence of causality in the world that it appears unthinkable that anyone should deny it. Yet men have denied it. There have been, and still are, those who assert that we can know nothing of the relation of objects and events except an *association* and *succession* which we have no right to call the relation of cause and effect. This means, for example, that when a piece of dry wood is thrown into a roaring fire, the fire is not to be called the cause, and the decomposition of the wood the effect, of the burning. Now, a treatise on Apologetics has neither the space nor the right to discuss this curious doctrine in detail. Only a general criticism of it can be offered to show that it is contradictory in theory and pernicious in its practical results.

First of all, it must be said that the existence of the cause-and-effect relation in the world is as evident as the existence of the world itself. Causality is understood by a direct and irresistible intuition of the mind, even as the bodily world is perceived by a direct grasp of the senses and of consciousness. All activity, all thought, goes forward upon the solid roadway of the recognition of the obvious fact of causality. The scientist in the laboratory, the surgeon in the operating-room, the physician at his work of diagnosis, the teacher in the classroom, the salesman dealing with a prospective buyer, the mechanic at work upon an automobile, the business man, the economist, the sociologist, the lawyer, the director of souls—all are seeking to know causes, or to produce effects, or to prevent undesirable effects. Everywhere and in everything we find causality showing itself inevitably in the activities of practical and intellectual life.

The man who denies causality denies all things; he must lapse into the endless silence of universal skepticism. Such a man has no right to take medicine for the relief of an ailment, nor to eat food to appease his hunger; to do these things would be to admit that the medicine could *cause* relief, and that the food could *cause* satisfaction of appetite. Nor has such a man even the right to defend his theory that there is no causality; for were he to offer argument, he would show that he believed argument capable of *causing* others to agree with him, and certainly such argument would reveal the reasons which *cause* him to hold his theory. Thus, the denial of causality is shown to be contradictory in theory. If the man who denies causality objects to this, if he says, "Between food and satisfied appetite, between medicine and the relief of sickness, between argument and mental conviction, there is only a relation of succession, albeit necessary succession," we answer, "Very well. You choose to call it a necessary relation; we call it cause; there is a difference in our terms, but not in the thing we mean." As a fact, those that deny causality dislike the word; they call it by another name; but they do not destroy the reality.

If there be no causality in the world, then the murderer is not the cause of his victim's death; the lazy student is not responsible for his failure in examinations; the good man deserves no praise for his virtues; the weakling is not to be encouraged, for he can in no wise amend his efforts. Thus the denial of causality is the denial of all practical morality. Hence, on grounds both speculative and practical, we reject the denial of causality as a contradictory and pernicious thing.

Causality, then, exists. There are really causes which contribute to the production of effects. Indeed, every object, every event in this finite world must have its cause or causes, and these must be *adequate,* i. e., sufficient to account fully for all the positive being or perfection of the effect. To limit our study to bodily objects—for our argument is to deal with this bodily or material world—we find that four causes regularly converge to produce a material or bodily thing. These causes are called, respectively, the *material,* the *formal,* the *efficient,* and the *final* cause. We shall study these as they are exhibited in a pertinent illustration:

1. I have on my desk a small marble statue of the Blessed Virgin Mary. This statue is neither infinite nor eternal, and hence it must have its causes; it is not a thing which *must* exist, but it has received existence from its causes. When I ask what these causes are, the first answer is obviously: the material, the stuff, out of which the statue is made. This is its *material* cause. It is a true cause, for without it the statue could not exist. The material cause of this statue is marble.

2. Now the statue might be made of wood, of plaster, of metal, or of other substance; but, as a

matter of fact, it is made of none of these things, but of marble. There is something that makes this substance the precise thing that it is; there is something that makes marble marble. This is a cause of the statue, for without it the statue would not be the precise kind of substantial thing that it is. This is the *substantial formal* cause of the statue.—Further, the statue has its outward shape, figure, or form. This is also a cause of the statue, for without it the statue would not be just what it is. This is the *accidental formal* cause of the statue. We use the term *accidental* to signify that which happens to be present as an extrinsic determination of the effect, although the effect would be essentially the same were this determination different. Thus, the statue would be a statue and a marble statue, even if it were of a different figure, or were made to represent some other personage than the Blessed Virgin Mary.

3. The statue has had a maker. The artist who produced it is its true cause. He is the *efficient* cause of the statue, for by his own activity he effectively produced it as this statue, using the material substance called marble to work upon.—The tools used by the artist in making the statue are also causes of the statue, for without them it could not have been made. These are *instrumental* causes of the statue. Instrumental causes are not major, but minor causes, for they subserve the action of the efficient cause.

—Further, the artist made the statue according to some plan or model (person, picture, sketch, image in his imagination, other statue, or the like), and this is also a cause of the statue, for without it the work of the efficient cause would not have been guided to produce just this statue. This is called the *exemplary* cause. Like the instrumental cause, the exemplary cause is a minor cause and subserves the action of the efficient cause.

4. The artist must have had some purpose, some end in view, in making the statue. Perhaps he made it to sell for money, perhaps he made it to express his devotion to the Blessed Mother, perhaps he merely wished to exhibit his skill, perhaps he only wanted to do something to pass away the time, perhaps he found pleasure in the work, perhaps several or all of these motives, or others, had a place in the work. In any case, the artist was moved to make the statue by some end in view which was recognized as desirable to achieve. Now, this end in view, or simply *end*, is a cause of the statue, for without it the efficient cause would not be stirred to make the statue. It is called the *final* cause of the statue (from the Latin *finis*, "end").

We see that of the four major causes two belong to the very being of the effect; they are *intrinsic* to the effect as such: these are the material and the formal cause. The other two causes, viz., the efficient and the final cause, are not part and parcel of the effect, but are *extrinsic* to it. Thus we divide the four causes as follows:

Intrinsic { Material (exists only for bodily effects)
{ Formal (substantial and accidental)

Extrinsic { Efficient (subserved sometimes by instrumental
{ and exemplary causes)
{ Final

In the argument which we are to offer presently we shall be concerned, first and foremost, with the necessity of admitting the existence of an efficient cause of the world. But first we have to consider another matter, one closely related to the question of efficient causality—indeed, it is a part of that question.

Everything that exists must have a sufficient explanation of its existence. Nothing can exist without a *sufficient reason* for its existence. Now, obviously this sufficient reason must be found either in the existing thing itself, or in that which gave it existence. To put the matter in another way: if a thing exists, then either (1) it is so perfect that it must exist and cannot be non-existent, or (2) it has received existence by the action of some efficient cause.

Now, if a thing be so perfect that it must exist and cannot be non-existent, it is *self-existent*. Such a thing contains in itself the sufficient reason for its existence. And since it must exist by reason of its own essential perfection, it has had no cause; it is eternal; it is *necessary* being (i. e., it necessarily exists), and not *contingent* upon the action of any producing cause.

If a being has received existence by the action of some efficient cause, it is not a *necessary,* but a *contingent* being, for it depends upon, is contingent upon, the action of its producing efficient cause.

Thus there are only two kinds of being possible: (1) eternal, uncaused, *necessary* being, and (2) *contingent* being, which is efficiently caused.

Further: contingent things, things efficiently caused, must be traced back to a first efficient cause, which is itself *necessary* and *uncaused* being. For consider: a contingent thing is a caused thing, its cause produced it. If its cause is also produced, something produced that cause, and so on. If A comes from B, and B from C, and C from D, and D from E, and E from F, and so on, then somewhere and sometime we must come to a *first* cause which is itself uncaused, which is *necessary* being. One cannot trace back the chain of causation indefinitely nor to infinity; one must really reach the beginning, one must really attain the knowledge of a necessary first cause. To say that the series is indefinitely long and to leave the matter there, is to make an intellectual surrender of the whole question, an unworthy surrender, which leaves the mind in precisely the same state as if no cause at all had been traced. Such a surrender is simply a refusal to face facts. On the other hand, to say that the series of causes is infinitely long (i. e., has no beginning) is to assert an absurdity. For an infinite number of finite causes is impossible; finite added to finite can never equal infinite. Reason forces us to the conclusion that contingent things involve of necessity the existence of an uncaused and necessary first cause.

Now, can there be *many* uncaused and necessary first causes? Can various chains of causation be traced back to various first causes? Or is the first cause necessarily *one* cause? We assert that the first cause is one and only one. For a being that is so perfect that it must exist must have the fulness of perfection, it must have perfection in a wholly unlimited manner. Why? Because such a being is *self-existent* and wholly independent of causes. Now causes do two things: they make an effect what it is, and they *limit* the effect so as to mark off its perfections from those of other things. Hence a being that is independent of causes, as a *necessary* being is, is independent of the *limitation* which causes impose. Thus the first cause is free from limitation; in other words, it is *infinite*. Now, an infinite being is unique; there simply cannot be more than one such being. For, if there were more than one, there would be a distinction of being between or among them; this distinction would be itself a limitation, and none would be infinite. Suppose, for example, that there are two infinite beings, A and B. A has its own per-

fections in an unlimited degree; B has its own perfections, similarly unlimited. Now, if A and B are
not identical (and thus *one*) there is a defect and a
limitation in A, inasmuch as it has not the perfections
that are properly B's. In like manner there is a defect
and a limitation in B, inasmuch as B has not the perfections that are properly A's. Thus, unless A and B
are identical and one, neither is infinite. We conclude
that there can be only one *necessary* being, because a
necessary being is infinite. Hence, the necessary first
cause must be *one* and *infinite*.

b) THE ARGUMENT

> Contingent things demand the existence of
> one, necessary, infinite first cause;
> Now, the world, and all things in the world,
> are contingent things;
> Therefore, the world, and all things in the
> world, demand the existence of one, neces-
> sary, infinite first cause. This we call God.

c) DISCUSSION OF THE ARGUMENT

The argument is set forth in what is called a *syllogism,* that is, three propositions so connected that,
when the first two are given, the third necessarily
follows. The first two propositions are called *the
premisses* of the syllogism; the last proposition is
called *the conclusion.* The first premiss is called *the*

major, and the second is called *the minor premiss.*

From what we have already learned about causality, it is evident that the major premiss is true.

The minor premiss asserts that the world and things in the world are contingent. This is not hard to prove. For the world is full of change, and wherever there is change, there is contingency. If things are *necessary,* if they must be what they are, and not otherwise, then change is impossible. Again, causes are required to produce change, and change is therefore *contingent* upon the action of such causes. Now, mundane things are subject to change, not only of quantity and quality and place, but of their very substance. Thus there is change from life to lifelessness, as when a living tree becomes a dead tree. There is change from dead matter to living matter, when, for instance, cooked meat is digested and becomes living tissue. Now, where such substantial changes exist, the very substances changed are contingent.—Again, limitation means contingency. For, as we have seen, limitation in being requires a cause. In other words, where being exists at all, it exists either independently of causes in an unlimited degree, or in that limited degree which actual causes give. Now, mundane things are obviously limited in space, in kind, in time or endurance, in quantity, in quality, etc. Hence, mundane things are caused; mundane things are *contingent* upon the action of causes. It is clear, then, that the minor premiss expresses an obvious truth: the world and all things in the world are contingent.

The conclusion of the argument is inevitable in view of the premisses; it follows necessarily from the premisses.

There is, therefore, a first cause of the world. From our remarks on causality and from the argument just discussed, we know that this cause is *one, necessary, infinite, eternal.* This Being, this First Cause, is God.

Here the cruder sort of evolutionist arises with a smile at our simplicity. He says, "All this talk of causality is well enough. But you go too far when you insist on having a first efficient cause necessarily existing in itself and acting as the producer of all things outside itself. This wonderful world of ours does not require so naïve an explanation. We find a sufficient explanation of the world in the almost incredibly long process by which the cosmic development has been actualized. There was, to begin with, some mass of world-stuff—call it nebula, call it matter, call it the field of force and energy—and as eons rolled away there emerged from this mass forms that began crudely to be differentiated. Time passed, tremendous stretches of it, and forms were more and more clearly developed; the cleavage of form from form was more definitely achieved. Then, as ages upon ages passed. . . ." Here we interrupt on our own account and ask, "What causes the original nebula or mass of world-stuff? It presents precisely the same problem as the world we see around us to-day. It is contingent, for it changes and develops; it must therefore have its cause, and its first cause; and this first cause must be eternal, one, infinite, necessary. Our argument remains untouched by your remarks. You cannot muddle us with your talk of ages and ages, and eons and eons. What has *time* to do with the question anyhow? Whether the world was made quickly or slowly cannot change the fact that it *was* made, that it demands its cause. You take as starting point the world as you think it once was; we take the world as it is; but we all take *the world* as starting point. And our argument is that one, eternal, infinite, necessary first cause is required for the world either as it is, or as, perhaps, it was."

SUMMARY OF THE ARTICLE

We have defined *cause, effect, causality.* We have seen that causality exists in the world as an indubitable fact. We have defined the four major causes of material things, viz., *material, formal, efficient, final,* and the minor causes that may subserve the action of the efficient cause, viz., *instrumental* and *exemplary* causes. We have centered our attention and framed our argument upon *efficient* causality in the world. We have seen that things efficiently caused are *contingent* upon their causes, and that such things demand, as a sufficient reason and explanation of their existence, a necessary being which is the *first* efficient cause. We have seen that the first efficient cause must be *eternal, one, necessary, infinite*. This first cause is God.

ARTICLE 2. THE ARGUMENT FROM MOTION

a) Doctrine of Motion   b) The Argument   c) Discussion
of the Argument

a) DOCTRINE OF MOTION

In the widest sense, *motion* is any activity, internal or external, bodily or spiritual, that can be exercised in a finite being. Thus, in this sense, there is motion in walking, in growing, in singing, in understanding, in making up one's mind.

In a more definite sense, *motion* may be defined as *the transition from potentiality to actuality.* This definition needs a word of explanation. A thing is *in potentiality,* inasmuch as it has the capacity to do or to receive something; and a thing is *in actuality,* inasmuch as such capacity is realized in fact. Thus, water is *actually* water (or is water in actuality), but *potentially* it is hydrogen and oxygen (or is hydrogen and oxygen in potentiality). Conversely, hydrogen and oxygen (taken in proportionate parts of two to one) are actually hydrogen and oxygen, but potentially these gases are water. In a word, a thing is actually what it is; potentially, it is what it may become. And what it may become may affect the thing in its very substance or in its accidents (i. e., quantity, quality, place, etc.). Thus, there is a transition from potentiality to actuality (and hence *motion*) when hot water becomes cold water, when a living body becomes a lifeless body, when a body is changed from one place to another.

In everyday speech the term *motion* conveys the idea of movement in space, or rather as the movement of a body from one place to another. This is *local motion,* or *locomotion.*

In whatever sense we choose to understand motion, we find that it is always a thing given, conferred, transmitted; it is never self-originating. Motion always requires two things: the *thing moved,* and the *mover* or *motor.* Motion requires a mover that is not one and the same as the thing moved. *Whatever is moved is moved by something other than itself.* This is a law that has no exceptions. Lifeless matter is inert and cannot move itself: living things "move themselves," but not in the sense that they are the complete origin and source of their motion, for they require a creator, a conserver, and the concurrence of their conserving cause in their activities or motions. Perhaps a further word on this matter is in order.

Lifeless things are inert and do not move themselves. Iron filings that move towards a magnet are not self-moving; they are moved by a power residing in the magnet. Nor does this power give itself origin and activity, but comes from another source. A steam engine "moves" or, rather, is moved, because steam forces the pistons back and forth, and these move rods that move wheels. Nor is the force of steam self-originating. Steam is given reality and power by the action of fire upon water. Nor have fire and water their force of themselves, but depend upon their constituent elements, and these upon other things, and ultimately upon the *first* cause, which gives all being.

Living things move themselves in accordance with set laws of nature (plants) and also in accordance with instinct aroused by sense-knowledge (brutes), and also by free choice exercised after the field of choice is manifested by intellectual knowledge (men). But no living thing gives itself life, the power of self-motion. Nor does a living thing preserve itself in being and activity. Its being and its motion depend ultimately upon the first cause, which is thus also the first mover. A man's senses perceive objects; but there must be objects there to perceive, else the senses are not stirred or moved to activity. A man's mind understands truths, but understanding depends upon sense-knowledge for its beginnings, and sense-knowledge depends upon external objects of sensation. Thus neither sensation nor understanding is self-originating, but both are dependent upon an inner life-principle (which did not make itself) and upon objects of knowledge (which did not make themselves). Wherever we find motion, we find that it is *stirred* into being by something other than the thing which is moved. Thus we have a universally true dictum in the law, *"Whatever is moved is moved by something other than itself."* When we speak of things less than the infinite first cause, we use the term "move" in a loose sense; we should properly use the passive voice and say, "is moved" and "are moved."

Now, if everything moved requires a mover, it is obvious that there must be a beginning of the chain of motion, there must be *a first mover,* which is really *first,* and is therefore *not moved itself* by some other thing. In other words, the fact of motion requires as a sufficient explanation, a sufficient reason for its existence, *a first mover itself unmoved.* For there cannot be an infinite series of movers or motors. If A is moved by B, and B by C, and C by D, and D by E, and so on, there *must* be a first beginning of the chain of motion, and of all such chains of motion. For the first mover must be *one,* since, being truly the *first* mover, it is not subject to the *cause* of motion, i. e., is not subject to *another* mover; it causes motion but is itself uncaused; it must be identified with the first cause of all things, the one and infinite God. If the first mover were distinct from the first and infinite cause of all things (which, as we have seen is *one*), then this *first mover* must be the creature of that first and infinite cause, and so it is not *first* at all, but *is moved* into being by the first cause.

b) THE ARGUMENT

> If there is motion in the world, there is a mover, and ultimately a first mover, itself unmoved;
> Now, there is motion in the world;
> Therefore, there is a mover, and ultimately a first mover, itself unmoved. This we call God.

c) DISCUSSION OF THE ARGUMENT

The first statement (the major premiss) is obvious in view of what we have learned in discussing the nature of motion and its adequate explanation.

The second statement (the minor premiss) is also evident.

There have been philosophers (of whom Protagoras, Greek philosopher of the fifth century B. C., is the most notable) who asserted that we need not look for the origin of motion, since everything *is* motion. "Nothing *is*," they say, "all is *becoming*." This doctrine is self-contradictory. It asserts that everything is in a perpetual state of flux, change, motion; and if this be so, all things are *contingent,* and the universal moving mass does not explain itself, but still demands a first cause. Thus there *is* need to look for the origin of motion. Again: in the very idea of movement or motion there is the notion of something new being continually acquired, and of something left behind, by the moving thing. Movement means the leaving of one state of being for another, the leaving of potentiality for actuality. Now, a thing cannot give itself what it does not possess; the new and perpetually renewed acquisitions or actualities must be given by something other than the thing moved. Nor can moving things progress in a circular series, passing mutations around a universal ring, unless there is a Supreme Unmoved Being outside the ring to originate and sustain the motion. In no case, not even in the absurd supposition that the "becoming theory" is true, can reason escape the conclusion that motion requires a first mover itself unmoved.

We need not pause to investigate in detail the doctrine of the old Eleatics (Greek philosophers of the sixth and fifth centuries B. C.) that there is no motion in the world. If that be true, then there is no validity in human knowledge. By our senses we perceive motion; by our minds we understand its presence and nature; and if there be no motion, then senses and the mind are deceived about one of the most evident facts in the world, and cannot be trusted at all. If there be no motion, there can be no real births or deaths, no growing up, no growing old. There is no need then for the motorist "stalled" on the railway crossing to fear the onrushing train; there is no occasion for planting crops which cannot grow; there is no possibility of taking the food which could not, in any event, be digested. And, since the denial of motion involves, as we have seen, the denial of the validity of human knowledge, there is no occasion to speak of reasons or arguments in support of the theory which denies motion: for, in the hypothesis, men's minds cannot be trusted to know whether such reasons and arguments are valid or foolish. Denial of motion involves denial of human reason; it involves an intellectual short-circuit; there remains but darkness, nescience, and "the rest is silence."

SUMMARY OF THE ARTICLE

In this Article we have defined *motion* and have explained various senses in which the term may be understood. We have investigated the law, *Whatever is moved is moved by something other than itself,* and we have seen that this "something other" must be traced back to a first mover itself unmoved, which is identified with the first cause itself uncaused. And this first mover is God.

In the preceding Article we learned that God, the First Cause, is *one, infinite, eternal, necessary.* In the present Article we learn that God is also unmoved and unmovable, i. e., that God is *immutable.*

ARTICLE 3. THE ARGUMENT FROM DESIGN

a) Meaning of Design   b) The Argument   c) Discussion
of the Argument

a) MEANING OF DESIGN

A *design* is, in simplest language, a *plan*. A plan
may exist in fancy or in intention; it may be expressed in a sketch of work to be done; it may stand
revealed in the structure and function of an already
existing thing. Thus, an architect's conception of a
projected building is his design or plan; so also are
his drawings; and the finished building exhibits in
itself the plan or design of its builder.

Here we discuss the plan of the world around us.
The world exists; it is not merely projected as a
thing to be made; it must exhibit in itself the design
of its maker.

But has the world a plan? Is it not, perhaps, a haphazard mass of matter, a jumble of objects thrown
together by accident? In a word, is it not possible
that the world has been arranged by *chance?* No, it
is not possible. *Chance* is an empty word in this connection. Chance cannot produce anything, nor the arrangement of anything. If chance could produce anything, it would be a cause but, obviously, chance is the
opposite of cause. If chance were a cause, its effect
would follow logically from it, and would not happen
by chance at all. Thus, to posit chance as cause is to involve oneself in a very evident contradiction. Of

course, even if the world were a jumbled mass of objects, it would still require its cause; and its arrangement, its very jumbled arrangement, would still require its cause. For if arrangement requires a cause, so does disarrangement; and *chance*—that tricky word—cannot be the cause of either.

We use the word *chance* in daily speech, as when we say, "We met by chance," or "It chanced to be raining." But this use of the word is very different from that of the pseudo-philosopher who employs it to explain the world. In the expressions quoted, we mean that a meeting (which had its *cause* in the persons who met and in their choice of paths) was *unforeseen* or *unintended;* and that the rain (which had its cause in atmospheric conditions) was *unexpected,* or was a *mere circumstance* in the situation or event described. Thus we use the word *chance* as a loose equivalent for that which is unexpected, unforeseen, unforeseeable, unintended, circumstantial, unimportant. So we speak of a chance meeting, a chance occurrence, a game of chance (in which the outcome is not to be foreseen), etc. We never really use the word *chance* as *cause;* indeed, in every case, the term is applied to an unexpected or unintended or circumstantial *effect*.

Granted, then, that chance cannot explain the world's arrangement, may we not still maintain that the world (which has, of course, its adequate cause) is without design, without plan? Not if we are in our five wits, and if we look at the world. For all about us we see *regularity* and *order,* and these are the soul of design. So obvious is the wonderful arrangement and order of the world that the ancient Greeks called it a *cosmos,* that is, a well-ordered thing; and the Romans could find no more suitable name for the universe than *mundus,* which means *clean and orderly.* There is regularity in the movements of earth and planets, in the constancy of types and species of living things, in the structure and arrangement of crystals in mineral substances. Scientists talk of physical, chemical, biological laws; and every one of these *laws* is a formula which expresses the constant, uniform order and regularity of objects and processes in the world. As well might one think to read the sonnets of Shakespeare printed in the dust by a handful of type scattered at haphazard, as to think that the marvellous regularity and order of the universe is without design.

To choose but a single example from a world of order—what wondrous arrangement and design is found in the structure of a simple plant. Here we have fine and delicate organs, each serving its purpose steadily and with admirable exactitude, and all harmoniously conspiring to produce flower, and fruit, and seed that will germinate and produce other fertile plants of the same kind.

Order means more than regularity of arrangement and function; it means a regular arrangement made with a view to some end, the serving of some purpose. This we find unmistakably in the world. The parts of a plant are not merely prettily arranged; they are arranged in a manner suitable to the requirements of the plant for life, growth, and germination. The eye of an animal is not only skilfully constructed; it is constructed to serve the purpose of seeing. The regular movement of earth and sun is not only a splendid and constant reality; it serves a great purpose, for it provides periods of light and heat, of rest and darkness, without which nothing could live and grow. The earth and its order serves the needs of men: the earth is fitted to be man's home and his workshop; man breathes the air of heaven; the clear waters of the earth slake his thirst; plants, animals, and minerals furnish him with food, clothing, shelter, warmth, and means for the development of mental and bodily powers in invention, research, construction. Thus there is order everywhere about us, order which is *arrangement with a purpose,* order which is the expression of *design.* The telescope and the microscope have revealed wonders in the universe, large and small; and whether we look out into the vast reaches of space or study the smallest particles of matter through magnifying lenses, we are everywhere confronted with a marvellous harmony, regularity, arrangement, order. In a word, we are confronted with applied design.

For, where there is order, there is necessarily de-

sign. And where there is design, there is infallibly a
designer. And where there is a designer, there is
an intelligent force. This reasoning is as incontrovertible as it is simple and direct. Further: the more
wonderful the design, the more wonderful is the intelligence of the designer. What a wondrous intelligence, then, has designed this great world, in general structure and in smallest detail; in the wide
sweep of cosmic movement and in the slightest at-
traction and cohesion of particle with particle; in
things lifeless and things alive; in the amazing har-
monies and bewildering complexities of living cells
and tissues; in the incredible function of generation;
in the miracles of speech, of reasoning, of free-will!
Dare we call it an intelligence less than infinite which
planned this world? Dare we call that power less than
limitless which carried the plan into execution?

Even if the marvel of the world did not force us
to conclude that an infinite intelligence designed the
world and an infinite power executed the design, we
should find our way to the same conclusion marked
out by cold reason. For consider: if the intelligence
which designed the world be other than the First
Cause, God, then that intelligence is an effect, a creature of the First Cause. And, since the effect receives
its being and all of its perfections from its adequate
cause, the intelligence which designed the world must
have received all its being and perfection from God,
and thus God is ultimately the intelligence that

planned the world. The same line of reasoning demonstrates the fact that it is the power of God which executed the world's design. Hence, that which is *first*, is *always* first: in causation, in conferring motion, in making and executing design. And, since the first Being is *infinite*, i. e., limitless in all perfection, it follows that the first Being is infinite intelligence and infinite power, or, in other words, is *omniscient* and *omnipotent*.

b) THE ARGUMENT

> *1.* If the world exhibits a most wonderful and constant order, it has a most wonderful and intelligent designer; nay, its designer must, in the last analysis, be the infinite First Cause or God;
>
> Now, the world exhibits a most wonderful and constant order;
>
> Therefore, the world has a most wonderful and intelligent designer; nay, its designer must, in the last analysis, be the infinite First Cause or God. Hence, God exists.

> *2.* The execution of a design of such marvellous complexity and perfection as the design of the world, demands, in the last analysis, the exercise of infinite power;

Now, the exercise of infinite power is the exercise of the power of God;

Therefore, the execution of the design of the world demands the exercise of the power of God. Hence, God exists.

c) DISCUSSION OF THE ARGUMENT

The first statement (the major premiss) of the first syllogism is evidently true in view of our preliminary discussion of design.

The second statement (the minor premiss) of the first syllogism is also obvious.

The conclusion follows of necessity.

In the second syllogism, the major premiss is evidently true; for the same process of reasoning that leads us to the knowledge of an infinite intelligence in the designer of the world, leads us also to the knowledge of an infinite power in the executor of the design.

The minor premiss of the second syllogism is equally evident. There can be only one infinite being, as we have already proved, and this we call God.

The conclusion of the syllogism follows of necessity from the premisses.

An objection may be raised. One may say, "There are imperfections in the world, and where there are imperfections in design and execution, it seems that there must be defects in the designer and executor.

Hence, the designer of the world cannot be of infinite intelligence and power."

Before answering this objection, let us be clear about the meaning of the term *perfection*. If a being has no limitations whatever, no deficiencies, no lack of all possible and thinkable actuality, then it is *absolutely* perfect. Obviously, an absolutely perfect being is infinite; and, since the infinite is necessarily one, there can be but one absolutely perfect being. The perfection of other things—things which come ultimately from the infinite First Being and First Cause —is *relative* perfection, that is to say, such things are measured as perfect or imperfect in *relation* to their fitness or unfitness to serve the end or purpose for which they were made. In other words, such things are perfect or imperfect inasmuch as they are fit or unfit to do the thing for which they were *designed*. Now, the world, notwithstanding what are called its imperfections, is admirably suited to the attainment of the end for which it was designed. Therefore, while it is not *absolutely* perfect (an impossibility, for the world is not infinite), it is *relatively* perfect.

It is no denial of the infinite power of the First Cause to say that it cannot create another infinite thing, i. e., an absolutely perfect thing. For a plurality of infinities is a contradiction; and infinite intelligence and power would be self-contradictory, it would simply not be infinite, if it could produce another infinity. Besides, the idea that a perfect cause must always produce the best thinkable effects is not justified. Must all the works of an agent (i. e., actor, doer, performer) be measured by the *full* power of the agent? Must every effect contain *all* the perfection of its cause? Must a man who can lift five hundred pounds never lift less than five hundred pounds? Must the man who can spend a million dollars never spend a dime? Must the automobile that can be driven at ninety miles an hour never be driven at five miles an hour? Must God, then, merely because He can, make things better or more perfect than they are? These questions indicate the absurdity of the objection. Still God is infinitely wise, and we may truly say that the things He makes are indeed the *very best,* not in themselves, but *in relation to* the end they were designed to achieve. In a word, the world is not the *best* world, absolutely speaking; but it is *relatively* the best world.

Imperfections in the world are, of course, no argument at all against the existence of a designer. Indeed, imperfections cannot be known as imperfections unless there is a *standard* of perfection, a *design* in fact, with which these imperfections appear to be out of harmony. One cannot tell whether a piece of cloth is more or less than a yard, unless there is a recognized standard called a yard. Similarly, imperfections or irregularities cannot be known as irregular if there is no standard of regularity (*design*) with which they fail, or seem to fail, to conform. Imperfections are no argument against design; on the contrary, they are a proof of design. They are the exceptions that prove the rule, i. e., *the design.*

By imperfections in the world we usually mean such things as harsh climate, noxious plants and animals, ill-health, imperfect organic structure, waste lands, malarial swamps, wars, famines, plagues, poverty, etc. Many of these things are directly or indirectly due to the abuse of man's great gift of free-will; they are not to be ascribed to God; for God gave man free-will for the best and highest purpose (which is the achieving of Himself and eternal happiness), and He will not take away that gift; to do so would be to contradict Himself. Other imperfections (such as harsh climate, animals unfriendly to man, desert spaces on the earth, etc.) are, as imperfections, unintelligible unless we admit that some primal sin has blighted the earth. We shall see in a later Chapter that such a sin was indeed committed; we merely notice here that the material world itself bears evidence of the Fall. But these things called imperfections lose their character as imperfections, and even become relative perfections, when we consider that they are very useful, and some of them even necessary, to fallen man. Without hardship, without stimulus, without many and continual prods to the task of achieving his last end, man would quickly degenerate into the broken victim of his own disordered passions. The imperfections of the world afford occasion and opportunity for self-control, for penance, for stabilizing character; they stir man to bodily, mental, and spiritual effort, without which he would never develop his capacities and capabilities; they make possible the splendid things called "social virtues." Without sickness, affliction, worry, poverty, how should we know of such perfections as nobility of soul, spiritual stamina, heroism? How should we have experience of such fine and gracious things as practical charity, benevolence, generosity? Without the stress of trials and persecutions, how should we know the ennobling power of self-sacrifice and feel the glorious inspiration of martyrdom?

If the thought should strike us, "How can things external, such as mere harshness of climate, be of any value to man? How can such a thing be more or less than an imperfection pure and simple?" we may find much illumination in the following remarks of Mr. Hillaire Belloc (*On,* pp. 136–137): "If one could exactly balance all the things which one desires in a climate, I will tell you what would happen. One would lose three things, each more important than the last—energy, decent morals, and happiness. I suppose what one would exactly balance in a climate would be a sufficiency of moisture without discomfort, a sufficiency of light without loss of repose, and a sufficiency of heat without the breeding of noxious things. . . . Well, if one lived in such a climate, I say that one would lose energy and morals and happiness. They say that the mind turns inward when it suffers too much sorrow. That is true; but it remains alive. It turns inward also, but in a permanent *dead* fashion, when it has no stimulus at all."

Perhaps the most baffling of the imperfections of the world are those of organic deficiencies, malformations, and physical pain in brute animals. Well, if we deny the obvious fact of original sin and its effect upon the whole world, we are face to face with an unanswerable problem. But if we look upon the world as a place made for man alone, to be his temporary dwelling-place and workshop; a place that contains many splendid creatures other than man, but all made for man's use; a place, finally, that man's sin has blighted and disordered—we shall easily understand that all creatures made to serve man must show something of the result of the havoc that sin has wrought. And even these things serve man; in animal suffering and malformation, man can truly look upon a thing that sin has done, and he can learn to hate sin in himself and to avoid it. Nor, on the other hand, is animal suffering a pure misery to the animal; without pain and suffering animals would not know of their hurts or diseases, and would take no measures to protect themselves or preserve their existence. Rightly considered, the imperfections here discussed are in no sense an argument against the relative perfection of the world's design.

Evil and suffering in the world are problems insoluble only when looked at in themselves. For the mere materialist, the unbeliever, the man who looks for his best heaven here on earth, evil and suffering are indeed problems without solution. But for the man who does not refuse to look at human life as it is, and to see it, as it ought to be seen, *against the background of eternity,* the problems do not present insuperable difficulty. Those who look at the world's imperfections *in themselves,* are like men who should consider a painful operation in itself and without reference to the thing called health and strength. There are such things as unpleasant means, but these may become endurable and even highly desirable in view of an important end which they will help to achieve. And so they may very properly be permitted to enter into the design that is directed to the attaining of that end.

It is the part of a wise and skilful designer to plan his work in such a way as to make it a suitable and useful means to the end it is intended to attain. How much wiser and more intelligent is the designer who, when his original work is blighted and broken, can quickly adapt the wreckage to serve as well as ever. How infinitely wise is the designer who has the intelligence and power to make the injured work serve *better than ever* in view of the new conditions of those that the design is to serve;—and such a designer is the Designer of this world.

Leaving the very interesting question of "imperfections" in the world, let us turn our attention to another matter. Sometimes even learned men are unbelievably dull, and in such moments they are likely to think that the Argument from Design is invalid if: (1) they can produce by art some of the things produced naturally in the world, or (2) if they happen to know the mere *names* that men have invented for physical and chemical elements found in the make-up of things in the world. Thus, it is possible to produce, by means of art, true diamonds, although, as a matter of fact, the process is so elaborate and expensive that digging for the natural product and risking the chance of finding it in tried fields, comes rather cheaper; and besides, no diamonds of great size have as yet been produced artificially. But surely the diamond-maker *plans* his work; his *design* is, indeed, very elaborate. There is obviously no argument in the business which can throw doubt upon the design of the world. For certainly it is not logical to assert or to imply that, because man can design a thing now, it was not designed in the first place. The other point considered here is equally valueless as an argument against design in the world. A chemist once remarked, "Look at this fine apple. Do you know, I can tell you every element that this fruit contains. This is a thing that men of old could not do; but science brings progress; we make steady advance; the world gives up more and more of its secrets; we are not so likely to cry 'miracle' now as we were a while back; nor, indeed, are we so

ready to admit a divine plan and power in things."
If the learned chemist had but translated his verbali-
zation into significant speech, he would doubtless have
been astonished—and it is not too much to hope that
he would have been ashamed—at what he really said.
For what he said amounts to this : "I know the names
that men have given to several very mysterious things,
things which I cannot create or even begin to create,
that are discovered in making an analysis of this
fruit. Of course, I do not know at all how these things
came together to make this fruit, nor do I understand
how they got the power to associate together, nor of
what essence they are. Indeed, I only know their
names. Yet, I feel that knowing these names is a
reason for denying design in the world." Now, no
sane man would make a statement of this kind, in
these words. But many a sane man, many a scientist,
many an educator, is making just such statements
every day, but he is "winding them about with circumstance," he is using words like *science,* and *progress,* and *enlightenment,* and *modern advance,* and
contemporary state of knowledge, and such terms,
terms that lend a kind of dignity and ponderous sen-
tentiousness to his utterance. Truly, "the world is
still deceived with ornament," and it is largely the
ornament of ornamental language. A simple but adequate answer might be made to the chemist—although the Sir Oracle of the Upstart School is sure
to find it *naïve,* and to admit the fact with a charm-

ing smile—in this wise: "You know what makes this apple. Suppose you construct one like it. Be sure to put seeds into it, seeds of your own wise making that will germinate and produce fruitful apple-trees." And one might add: "Do this *without design.*"

There is much to be learned from what the pompous sciolist would call "nursery examples." Let us consider one. Suppose a watchmaker should give you a little white box, telling you that it is filled with a liquid substance, instructing you to keep it in a high, even temperature for twenty-one days, and assuring you that, at the end of that time, you would find in the box a splendid watch, with wheels, balances, jewels, face, hands, stem, case, all complete. You would not think the watchmaker sane. But suppose the experiment worked out as he said. Then, indeed, you would be forced to acknowledge him as the most wonderful and skilful watchmaker ever known in the world's history. What a power, what an intelligence must be his who could design the elemental liquid and cause it to develop by such simple means as the application of heat into an intricate timepiece! Now, let the little white box of the watchmaker be replaced by an ordinary fertile egg. Here is a little white box filled with liquids. Keep it in a warm place for a few weeks, and what is the result? A thing a million times more wonderful and intricate than any watch. There will come from this little white box a creature that is *alive;* finished to the last detail of beak and feather; furnished with eyes of marvellous construction and mysterious power, capable of feeling, of hearing, of moving about; capable of finding food, though uninstructed; capable of transforming dead food into living tissue of muscle, nerve, and bone; made in such wise that part fits perfectly to part in an organism of the most intricate arrangement and the most complex and delicate balance. Here is plan, here is design, here is power!

When we hear large and learned talk of *nature,* and *energy,* and *force,* and *adaptation,* and *environment,* and *behavior,* and *heredity,* and *transmitted variations,* and all the sounding litany of scientific and pseudo-scientific terms, let us remember that names are names and nothing more. Anyone can paste on a label. We may call life by the name of *biotic force* or *plasmic energy* if we like; but we do not change the thing called life by giving it a Greek name; nor do we explain life merely by calling it something else. So with the things in this world. Call them by what learned names we will, our learning does not explain them, nor does it take away their designer. The universe, however named, still proclaims its design and its most intelligent, most powerful designer.

In the arguments so far developed we have learned, by sheer reasoning, that there is a First Cause of the world and all things in it, and that this First Cause is *eternal, one, infinite, necessary, immutable, omnis-cient, omnipotent.* We may add another attribute to the list: the First Cause is perfectly *free.* For, if the First Cause is one, is alone, what is there to *force* its action? And self-forcing is unthinkable, for it involves a limitation in the *infinite* (and hence *non-limited*) First Cause. Therefore, the idea of force or compulsion affecting the First Cause and requiring its action is self-contradictory; and it follows that the First Cause is perfectly free in producing its effects. This most perfect First Cause we call by the name *God.*

SUMMARY OF THE ARTICLE

In this Article we have defined *design* and have studied its obvious presence in the world. We have seen that *chance* can never be a *cause* of anything, but is only an accident or a circumstance of an *effect.*

From the order and design of the world we have concluded by direct reasoning to the existence of a designer. We have seen that this Designer must be of boundless intelligence and power.

The Argument from Design is often called *The Teleological Argument,* a name derived from the Greek word *telos,* which means *end.* For a thing designed is designed to attain a purpose or *end;* where there is design, there is inevitably an end to be reached by the design.

ARTICLE 4. THE ARGUMENT FROM THE MORAL ORDER

a) Meaning of the Moral Order   b) The Argument
c) Discussion of the Argument

a) MEANING OF THE MORAL ORDER

By *the moral order* we mean the department of the world's activity that is marked with the character of *morality,* that is, which is right or wrong, good or bad. In a word, *the moral order* means the free and deliberate activity of human beings. All human conduct which is deliberate and free belongs to *the moral order.*

Man, in his free and deliberate acts, is conscious of an obligation. He inevitably knows that there is a duty upon him and a prohibition: he knows that he must *do good* and *avoid evil.* He recognizes an order in things that he is bound to conserve and forbidden to disturb. All men, in a word, feel clearly and know unmistakably that their activities are subject to *a law.* Now, this is not a physical law like the law of growth or the circulation of the blood, laws which man cannot disobey; this is a law which governs by suasion and not by force or coercion; it is a law which men are physically free to disobey, but which their understanding cannot disregard. This law is called the natural law; it is a *moral* law which indicates to man what he *ought* to do, but does not *force* him to do it.

We say that a man's *conscience* (i. e., reason recognizing and pronouncing upon matters of good and evil, right and wrong) makes him aware of the moral law. This fact is universally true. All men of all times, savages and cultivated peoples, have come to a knowledge of right and good to be done, and of evil and wrong to be avoided, as they come to the "use of *reason.*"

Now, among varied peoples there may be various *applications* of the moral law, but the law itself is everywhere and always the same, viz., "Do good; avoid evil." If at times there exist odd and varying notions of just *what* is good and *what* is evil, human weakness and human perversity (evidence of the Fall!) explain the diversities. But there are no diversities among men even in applications of the moral law in obvious matters. No man of any race or tribe ever believed that murder, lies, contempt of parents, are good things; no man ever thought that love of parents, truthfulness, honesty, are evil. It is no objection to this statement to assert that the Roman father believed he had the right of life and death over his children and his slaves, and that he sometimes killed them. This is not saying that the Roman approved of murder; it is only saying that he did not regard as murder the killing of his children or slaves. The Carthagenian mothers who threw their infants into the flames in the horrible worship of Moloch, did not regard murder as good; they regarded sacrifice to

Moloch as no murder. The wrong view of Roman
and Carthagenian was a perverse and mistaken application of the moral law; it was not a failure to
recognize a moral law at all. Was not the idea of
parental authority a recognition of moral law; was
not the sorry idea of an obligation to worship Moloch
a moral idea?

There is a law then which imposes itself upon man's
consciousness, and he feels its obligation even when
he does not obey it in action. Whence comes this
law? Man does not make it for himself, for it often
forbids what he wants to do, and commands what he
would be glad to avoid: his wishes make no change in
the law, as they certainly *would* if he were its author.
Nor can the moral law be explained by saying that
it is a mere outgrowth of custom among men. A custom can be changed; but reason asserts that the moral
law cannot be changed. Reason revolts at the idea of
murder being made a virtuous act, of men giving
thanks for the privilege of having their property
stolen, of mothers rejoicing in the shame of their
children; and yet reason would have no impulse to reject these things if the view that they are wrong were
merely a habitual point of view, a custom. Finally,
laws passed by kings and senates—*human legislation,* in a word—cannot explain the moral law and
the knowledge of man that there are things good and
things evil. For human laws can be abrogated; new
laws can be passed; and if human laws are the source

of the moral law, the moral law can be changed.
Statute books may come to justify murder and to
make theft a virtuous act; but the human mind will
never be able to regard murder as good and theft as a
virtue. We are forced by the irresistible evidence of
reason, of common sense, to reject the idea that the
moral law comes from man himself, or from custom,
or from human legislation.—The question still remains: *Whence comes the moral law?*

The moral law is, first and foremost, a true *law*.
Hence it must, of necessity, come from a *lawgiver*.
This lawgiver (who is not man himself, nor man's
ancestors) obviously must have the intelligence to
frame the moral law, the right and power to impose
it, and the wisdom to enforce it. This legislator we
call *God*.

It is obvious, of course, that the Supreme Legislator and the First Cause of the world must be one and
the same reality. For if the Legislator be distinct
from the First Cause, then the Legislator is an effect of the First Cause, proximate or remote, and his
intelligence, right, power, come from, and are ultimately to be ascribed to, the First Cause. And, further, it is clear that the First Cause of the world,
being supremely intelligent and powerful (as we have
proved in another place), must have had a plan and
design that He willed to have carried out; it is obvious that the First Cause has established a course
for the attainment of His purpose; and such a course

must take the form of coercion or force for lifeless things and for living things devoid of freedom; it must take the form of *the moral law* for creatures whose activities are under their own control and within their own choice.

b) THE ARGUMENT

> There exists in the consciousness of all men the inevitable knowledge of a universal law, changeless and absolute, which requires the free-will (though it does not *compel* or *force* it) to do good and to avoid evil;
>
> Now, such a law presupposes the existence of a lawgiver, distinct from and superior to man's nature and will, who is ultimately identified with the First Cause, God.
>
> Therefore, God exists.

c) DISCUSSION OF THE ARGUMENT

The first statement is evident in view of what has been said in discussing the moral order. The moment a man ceases to be an infant, the moment he "comes to the use of reason," as the saying is, that moment he recognizes certain things as good and certain things as evil; and he realizes an obligation incumbent upon him of doing the good and avoiding the evil things. Not all things, indeed, but *certain* things are clearly known as *good in themselves* (and so to be done or at least permitted), and other things are known as *evil in themselves* (and hence forbidden). The coming "to the use of reason" is not a sudden recognition of these things, but a gradually clarifying knowledge of *some* of these things; and as life and experience continue, the actual number of such things normally increases in one's knowledge; but *the moral law itself* (i. e., "Do good; avoid evil") is clearly known from the moment a person "becomes responsible" for his conduct. This is a requirement of rational nature: hence the moral law is truly *universal:* it is recognized by all normal men of all times. And, further, the moral law is *changeless,* as we have amply shown above. Finally, the moral law is *absolute,* as human consciousness and experience testify. "Absolute" means "unconditional." Conscience does not say, "Do good, if you like; avoid evil, if you please." Conscience says simply, "Do good; avoid evil," without reference to human likes or pleasures. Similarly, in its individual mandates or applications, the moral law is absolute. Conscience says, "Do this; shun that"; it does not say, "Do this, if you find it convenient; avoid that, unless you dislike doing it." There is no condition or qualifier attached to the mandates of the moral law; it is *absolute.*

The second statement of the Argument is a simple requisite of reason. Effect demands an adequate cause; if there is a law, there is a lawgiver. That the lawgiver is distinct from man's own nature, man's will, is obvious; else man could change the moral law and free himself of its obligation without any sense of guilt. That the lawgiver is superior to man's nature and will, is obvious from the fact that man is constrained to recognize himself as the *subject* of the law, as under the direction of the lawgiver.

The conclusion follows logically from the premisses.

SUMMARY OF THE ARTICLE

In this Article we have seen that there exists a moral order, an inevitable classification of free human acts as good and evil. We have indicated the existence of the moral law, which demands the performance of good acts and forbids those that are evil. All men are forced by their rational nature to admit both that the moral law exists and that they are subject to it. We have seen that the moral law cannot come from man himself, nor from long-established custom, nor from human legislation: in a word, this law cannot come from any merely human source. Men are subject to this law; it must, therefore, come from a superhuman source. We conclude that there is an original Lawgiver (who is God Himself, the First Cause), independent of and superior to man's will.

ARTICLE 5. THE ARGUMENT FROM HISTORY

a) Value of Universal Human Consent   b) The Argument
c) Discussion of the Argument

a) VALUE OF UNIVERSAL HUMAN CONSENT

When all men of all times agree upon the existence of a certain fact, we say that there is a *universal human consent* in the matter upon which they are agreed. The word *consent* is used here in its original Latin meaning of *agreement* or *common feeling*. Even though, here and there, individual men or groups of men prove the rule of such consent by exception, we still call the consent or consensus *universal*.

Now, of what value is this universal consent? Does it necessarily express truth? Is there not at least a possibility of such consent being erroneous?

The universal consent of mankind *in matters that pertain to reason, or depend upon reason,* simply cannot be erroneous. Here the universal consent cannot be other than the voice of rational nature, and if *that* can be false, there is no longer any certainty in human reasoning at all, and we can know nothing for certain. Since we cannot contradict ourselves by the absurdity of absolute scepticism, we must declare that the voice of rational nature is an infallibly true voice.

But, it may be objected, all men once agreed that the sun moves around the earth. They were wrong, though their consent was truly universal. Hence, the universal consent of mankind is valueless as a test of truth. This objection does not touch our position at all. Men wrongly judged the movement of the sun —a physical fact. This was not a judgment belonging to the rational order; it was not a deduction of reason; it was a precipitate opinion based on mere external appearances. It is quite possible for many men or for all men to be wrong in such a judgment; but it is quite impossible for all men to be wrong in the conclusions reached by right reason upon known facts. Men may be wrong in judging the motion of the sun; they cannot be wrong in judging that motion requires a mover. Men may be wrong in judging, from mere appearances, that a certain triangle is equilateral; they cannot be wrong in concluding that the angles of a triangle equal 180°.

In the present Article we speak of the universal consent of mankind as a *reasoned conclusion* from known facts and experiences of life. God is not seen in the sky like the sun; God is not observed by the senses like the heat of a summer day. There is no possibility of universal error due to the precipitate judgment of mankind about God as about a physical fact observable by the senses. But sky, and earth, and heat, and stars, and men, and beasts, and all things existing in the world are known facts, and reason requires that they have an explanation sufficient to account for their existence. Thus, it is a reasoned judgment that declares the existence of a First Cause, a First Mover, a First Designer, a First Lawgiver. And

while the reasoning process is often obscure and in-
articulate, it is indeed a true reasoning process that
leads men to the knowledge of God, and not a hasty
judgment upon observed phenomena. A universal
reasoning process leads to a single universal consent
regarding the existence of God. In such a judgment
the universal consent of mankind cannot be false, else
there is no trusting reason at all, there is no truth to be
known for certain about anything.

b) THE ARGUMENT

> That which is declared by the universal con-
> sent of mankind as a judgment of rational
> nature, must be true;
> Now, the existence of God is declared by the
> universal consent of mankind as a judg-
> ment of rational nature;
> Therefore, the existence of God must be true.
> God exists.

c) DISCUSSION OF THE ARGUMENT

The first statement (the major premiss) is certain in view of our remarks upon the value of universal human consent.

The second statement (the minor premiss) is supported by the evidence of all history; and this, by the
way, is the reason for calling our present argument,
The Argument from History. The study of languages
(philology) shows that all historic peoples have had
a name for God. Monuments and temples, priesthoods

and sacrifices, festivals and sacred rites, testify to the incontrovertible fact that some idea of divinity has always and everywhere been in the mind of man. Writers of all eras, travellers, archaeologists, and historians are at one in their testimony that no people or tribe ever existed without some notion of a deity. The idea of divinity is inevitably bound up in nature; and the conclusion that God exists is directly reasoned from the facts and experiences of life. The voice of nature proclaims the existence of the Author and Ruler of nature. Even belief in false gods, in many gods, in monstrous gods, is still a belief (however perverted) in divinity; and behind all such beliefs, behind the notion of many gods, there has always been, as Mr. G. K. Chesterton so well says, "the idea of one God, like the sky behind the clouds." Men cannot escape the knowledge that there is an originator and ruler of the world. Their further conclusions may lead to false beliefs, like belief in many gods, but the *original* conviction is the reasoned conviction, and this is everywhere and always the same. It is with this conviction that our present argument deals.

The third statement (the conclusion) follows inevitably from the premisses.

SUMMARY OF THE ARTICLE

In this brief Article we have studied the value of universal human consent as the expression of infallible truth. We have learned that while many men, or even all men, may be wrong in their interpretation of mere physical facts, all men cannot be wrong in a judgment which is a direct inference of reason from known facts. *In a matter of rational inference, what all men of all times have everywhere known as true, must, as a matter of fact, be really true.* Such a universal agreement is the very voice of rational nature, and if it can be false, then there is no trusting reason at any time in any pronouncement, there is no certainty to be had in anything. To deny the validity of reason in this wholesale fashion is to involve one-self in self-contradiction. The man who says, "I still deny the value of your argument from universal human consent; as a matter of fact, there *is* no certainty to be had about anything," must find an answer to the reply, "Are you *certain* of that?" If no, then there is no certainty that there is no certainty. If yes, then there *is* certainty after all!

In plain matters of rational inference, therefore, certainty is to be had; and when all men agree upon such inference, error in their conclusion is unthinkable. Now such an agreement proclaims the existence of God. Therefore, God exists.

To conclude the Chapter on the Existence of God, we must make a brief study of *Atheism,* which denies God's existence, and of *Agnosticism,* which declares God's existence doubtful and a matter that can never be certainly known by man.

1. *Atheism* (from the negative or privative Greek particle *a* and the noun *theos,* "God") denies the existence of God. Those who profess Atheism as a doctrine are called *theoretical* or *speculative atheists,* while those who live as though there were no God, even though they profess belief in Him, are *practical atheists.* We speak here of theoretical or speculative Atheism.

Theoretical Atheism does not square with human reason. Reason demands the existence of God, as we have shown in various rational proofs of God's existence. Atheism does not offer a single telling argument against these proofs, nor can it offer positive argument for its claims. Atheism does not meet human needs; it conflicts with cold reason; it takes hope, courage, joy, and love out of the heart; it renders futile the desire for happiness which is ineradicably implanted in every human soul. Further, atheism destroys morality; for if there is no God, there is no supreme judge of human conduct, no supreme legislator, no supreme law, no supreme sanction for law (i. e., no everlasting reward or punishment). Atheism also destroys authority, for all authority in the world is ultimately based upon the supreme authority of God.

It is doubtful whether there are, or ever have been, any thoroughly sincere and perfectly convinced theoretical atheists. Pride and perversity have led some men to deny God; the love of a following, and the

puerile pleasure of saying shocking and startling
things, have caused others to declare themselves
atheists. But when reason is allowed to function, and
is not throttled by vanity, pride, or perversity, men's
minds *must* recognize the existence of God. As a
matter of fact, all the most noble and enlightened men
of every age have openly professed their belief in
God.

2. *Agnosticism* (from the Greek *a* and *gnostikos*,
"knowing"—hence *not knowing, ignorant*) is the
doctrine that men *do not* know and *cannot* know
whether there is a God. This is at once a cowardly and
an impertinent doctrine. It is cowardly, because it is
a refusal to face facts; it is a doctrine suitable for
what is called, in the language of the streets, "a quitter"; it is a surrender to unfounded doubt; it is a
weak refusal to see facts and to trace them to their
source. It is an impertinent doctrine, for it declares,
with the saucy attitude of a spoiled child, that what the
"quitter" fails to do, other men are powerless to do.

Normal minds have no patience with agnosticism.
We all can respect honest doubt; but doubt about the
existence of God is not honest; if reason be employed,
certainty in the matter must be attained. An agnostic
is like a man who should say, with a silly and super-
cilious smirk, "Well, I won't go so far as to deny that
two and five make seven, but, after all, I don't know."

An agnostic is one who preaches a religion of darkness. He is not like a humble man who frankly says,

"I don't know where I am in this fog"; he is like the insanely proud man who cries with an air of demoniacal triumph, "Here I am in the fog; and here we all are!"

If one should say, "I am in some doubt whether South America exists," we should say, "There is a way to make sure; take that way." To the agnostic we say, "You pretend that no man can know whether God exists, but you shall not enslave our minds with that grotesque pretense. How do you *know* men cannot know? Produce your evidence, bring forward your proofs. Until you show reason, you cannot expect men to contradict reason for the pleasure of relying upon your unsupported word. Must men not say, 'I believe in God'; and must they say instead, 'I believe in the omniscient Agnostic'? If you thus deify yourself, give evidence of your divinity; give us proofs of your existence and your all-embracing wisdom. If you cannot do that, you are an impertinent upstart. As a matter of fact, there is a God. There is a way to make sure that there is a God; take that way, and leave your preaching of doubts."

Agnosticism, like atheism, upsets morality; for a doubtful God cannot be a certain judge of human conduct, the framer of certain law, the certain source of authority. Thus both atheism and agnosticism contradict reason and are pernicious in their practical results.

CHAPTER II

THE NATURE AND ATTRIBUTES
OF GOD

We have proved *that* God is. Now we are to study *what* God is. In this Chapter we seek to express, in general but quite definite terms, what God is in Himself; then we will investigate in some detail certain of the divine perfections. In other words, we are to study, first *the nature,* then *the attributes* of God.

The Chapter is divided into two Articles, as follows:

Article 1. The Nature of God
Article 2. The Attributes of God

Article 1. The Nature of God

a) Meaning of *Nature*   b) God's Nature

a) MEANING OF *NATURE*

By the *nature* of a thing we mean its essence considered as the root and source of its proper activities. Thus we say that thinking and reasoning is in accordance with the nature of man, that it belongs to the nature of fire to burn, that it is the nature of the eye to see colored objects, that it is natural for animals to move about, and so on.

When we observe an activity that is always and

everywhere characteristic of a thing, we have an index to the *nature* of that thing; we learn what a thing is from the manner in which it acts. Thus, by studying the characteristic activities of a thing we learn to define the thing itself, to declare just what sort of thing it is; to formulate, in a word, a definition *of its nature.*

b) GOD'S NATURE

The activity of God is made manifest to human reason through experience of the world around us. This experience shows us that there must be a *first cause, itself uncaused,* and that this must be a *necessary being.* This First Cause and Necessary Being is God. All this we have learned in the Chapter on God's existence. Here we study the matter further to find its implications, its fuller meaning, so that we may formulate a satisfactory definition of God, and state just what God's nature is.

1. God is *necessary* being; He cannot *not*-be; He must exist; existence belongs to His very essence. We conclude perforce that *God is Self-Existent Being.* Obviously, God is not *self-caused;* the term is a contradiction: it really means that a thing exists first and then gives itself existence—an obvious absurdity. God is not caused at all. He exists, not *from* Himself, but *of* Himself. He is *Subsistent Being Itself.* Now, since God is wholly uncaused, and since there is no causality at all which is not rooted in Himself, there

is nothing in God that is subject to the action of any cause. There is, in other words, nothing *potential* in God which the action of due cause could render *actual;* nor is there anything in God which can be reduced from actuality to potentiality through the operation of adequate cause. For the "due cause" and "adequate cause" of which we speak do not exist, nor is there anything in God that could be subject to their action if they did. In a word, there is nothing potential about God at all; *He is Pure Actuality;* He is the *Pure Actuality of Existence.*

2. Since God is the Pure Actuality of Existence, there is nothing conceivable that can be imagined as *added* to God, in such wise as to make Him greater or more perfect; nor can anything be thought of as *removed* from God, in such a way as to make Him less perfect. For, since God is not subject to causal action, there is no cause that could produce an increase or diminishment in Him. Again, even if there were such a cause it would have to come from God Himself, and God, subjecting Himself to its action, would be self-changed thereby. Now, self-change is as contradictory in a necessary Being as self-cause. Finally, only the absolute fulness, completeness, plenitude of being (i. e., of perfection) can *require* existence; and hence a necessary Being must have *the plenitude of all being.* Now, that which has absolute plenitude of being, which can neither be increased nor decreased in per-

fection, must be *infinite*. Therefore, God is *infinite,* or *infinitely perfect*. God's infinity or "limitlessness" in perfection is not a mere negation of limiting causes or boundaries; it is the *positive* fulness of being in pure and absolute actuality.

3. Obviously, there cannot be a plurality of infinite beings. An infinite being has the absolute fulness and plenitude of being. There is, so to speak, no being "left over" for another thing to possess of itself and in its own absolute right. If there were two infinite beings, there would be perfection proper to the first which the second did not possess, and similarly there would be the proper perfection of the second which would necessarily be absent from the first: as a fact, neither of the two "infinite beings" would be infinite. Therefore, it follows directly from the fact of God's infinity that He is *one God* and that there are *no others* equal to Him. God is the *one* and *only* God. This truth we express by the term *unity* of God.

4. Since God is infinite and uncaused, it follows that He is *simple,* i. e., not composed of parts or elements. In other words, God is not a *composite* or *compounded* being. Every composite being is contingent upon the union of its parts and requires a uniting cause to bring these parts into union. But in God there is neither contingency nor subjection to causality. Again, the parts of a composite being are logically or naturally prior to their union; and there is nothing

prior to the eternal God, the *necessary* First Cause. God, therefore, is *simple.* He has no *possessed parts or perfections;* His perfections are one with His undivided essence; all that God *has,* He *is.* Thus, properly speaking, God does not *have* wisdom; God *is* Wisdom. Wisdom is one with the infinite essence of God, and hence God is Infinite Wisdom. Similarly, God is Infinite Justice, Infinite Mercy, Infinite Power, etc.

5. Since God is simple, He is *spiritual.* For a real, subsistent being must be either bodily or spiritual. Now, a bodily being is always made up of bodily parts, is contingent upon these parts and upon their union, is *composite.* But, as we have seen, God is not composite, but simple. He is therefore not bodily; it remains that He is spiritual. And, being infinite in all perfection, He is a Spirit infinitely perfect.

To sum up: Our fundamental idea, our basic grasp of God is this: God is Self-Existent Being; He is Subsistent Being Itself. This is a *metaphysical* definition of God—metaphysical, because it consists of the essential realities that are understood to make up the very idea of God. In the *physical* order God is a real being, infinite and spiritual; and we express this fact in the physical definition of God: God is a Spirit infinitely perfect. In answer therefore to the question, *What is God?* we say:

God is Self-Existent Being; God is Subsistent Be-

ing Itself (the metaphysical essence of God, expressed in metaphysical definitions) ; or

God is Infinite Spirit; God is a Spirit Infinitely Perfect (the physical essence of God, expressed in physical definitions).

SUMMARY OF THE ARTICLE

In this Article we have discussed the meaning of *nature*. We have studied the nature of God, proceeding first to discover the content of the very idea or concept of a necessary being, and so we found the metaphysical essence of God and expressed this in a metaphysical definition. Then we studied the direct, objective nature of the Self-Existent Being, and found that this must be one, infinite, simple, spiritual ; so we found the physical essence of God and gave it expression in a physical definition.

Our reasoning in this Article has been somewhat involved, but it has been clear and inevitable. It is as incontrovertible as the reasoning which leads to the demonstration of a theorem in geometry. The Catholic apologist should appreciate the worth and dignity of this reasoning, and he should require his auditors to appreciate it. There is not a shred of sentiment about it, nor is it marked by deviousness or word-juggling. It is coldly scientific.

ARTICLE 2. THE ATTRIBUTES OF GOD

a) Meaning of *Attribute*   b) Attributes of Being   c) Attributes of Intellect   d) Attributes of Will

a) MEANING OF *ATTRIBUTE*

By an *attribute* or *property* of a thing we mean a perfection which belongs to the nature of the thing, but is no essential *part* or constituent *element* of the thing. Once a thing is perfectly constituted in its essence, and is not thwarted or impeded, it inevitably manifests its attributes. The attributes of a thing "flow out," so to speak, from the perfectly constituted essence of the thing. In other words, *the thing being what it is,* certain attributes follow. To illustrate: The Church is an institution founded by God-made-Man Himself to teach and govern men and lead them to salvation. *The Church being what it is* (i. e., *divinely* founded for a definite purpose), it follows that the Church cannot *fail* in that purpose, and cannot *teach men falsely.* In a word, the Church is indefectible and infallible: or, in other terms, the Church has the *attributes* of indefectibility and infallibility. To illustrate further: Man is a rational animal, and must exercise the function of thinking. Thinking is no *part* of man, but when a man's essence is fully and perfectly constituted, when its operations are not thwarted by immaturity, defect, unconsciousness, distraction, then inevitably a man must think. Thus thinking is an *attribute* of man. It is that which must be *attributed* to man as man : *man being what he is,* the attribute follows of necessity, and man is necessarily a thinking creature.

Attributes are distinctive of the thing to which they belong ; they are indices of a particular nature. Hence they are called *properties,* that is, they are *proper* to special natures. The sum-total of the attributes or properties of an essence is found connaturally joined with that essence alone. Thus, to know the attributes of an essence is to know *a nature.* To understand the nature of anything we study its attributes.

Attributes, then, are perfections possessed by a thing precisely because it is the kind of thing that it is. Now, we have seen that God is simple, and so God does not *possess* or *have* perfections distinct from Himself. God is one and indivisible, and all His perfections are of His essence : all that God *has,* God *is.* Properly speaking, therefore, God *has* no attributes. Still, it is impossible for the limited human mind to take a direct and all-embracing view of the unlimited God. Our study must follow a plan that *seems* to sever the divine perfections one from another and from the divine essence. In a somewhat similar manner, we are forced by our human limitations to study any great or majestic object in a fashion that may be called piecemeal. Thus we may look upon the stately Jungfrau ; we may view it from many angles ; each angle will give new impressions, new vistas of background, new shapes and contours : yet the mountain is a single peak. Surely, if we cannot behold even a bodily object on all sides in a single view; if we cannot have an understanding of any intellectual principle in all its actual and possible applications by one simple unstudied grasp of mind; then our unstudied view of the infinite God cannot be a single all-embracing vision or understanding. But let us keep clearly in mind, as we study the various attributes of God, that these are really not distinct from God, but are one with His undivided essence. God, in His very essence, is all that is perfect in limitless degree; for God is *simple* and *infinite*.

b) THE ATTRIBUTES OF GOD'S BEING

In discussing the Nature of God we have discovered His fundamental attributes, viz., His necessity, infinity, unity, and simplicity. Here we are to study certain other divine attributes.

The attributes of God that belong immediately to His Being as such, are His *eternity, immensity, ubiquity,* and *immutability.*

1. We indicate God's *eternity* when we say, "God always was and always will be." Since God has no perfection distinct from His essence, His eternity is one with Himself. God is necessary being, uncaused, without beginning or end. His existence does not protract itself through successive moments, days, years, centuries; it is wholly present in a single unending *now.* For God there is no past, no future, but an all-

embracing present, a single undying universal instant.—The proof of God's eternity lies in the fact of His necessity. A necessary being must exist, and cannot be non-existent; existence belongs to its very essence. Obviously, such a being is *always* a necessary being (else, it *began* to be necessary under action of some cause, and so is *contingent* and not necessary at all!); and being always necessary, it is always existent; in other words, it is *eternal.* And the proof that God's eternity excludes successive moments, excludes past and future, is evident from His infinity: for in succession there is always a loss and gain, the leaving of one moment's experience for the experience of the next succeeding moment; but that which is infinite cannot have increase or diminution, loss or gain.

2. We indicate God's *immensity* when we say that God is not limited by space. We do not mean that God is of vast *size,* for size belongs only to bodily things; we do mean that God is *immeasurable,* that He is not enclosed by spatial dimensions either in the existing universe or above and beyond it.—The proof of this point is found in God's infinity and simplicity. For *the infinite* is unlimited, and that which is measurable is limited by its dimensions. And *the simple* is undivided and indivisible, and that which is measurable is divisible into measurable parts, areas, or volumes.

3. We indicate God's *ubiquity* when we say, "God

is everywhere." As God's immensity means that He is not limited by *space,* so His ubiquity means that He is not limited to a certain *place.* God is present in every place, in every part of the existing universe. God is wholly and entirely present in every place, and this in such wise that He is not circumscribed or bounded by the boundaries of the place. God is wholly present in all the world and in all parts of the world, but He is in no wise identified with the world.—The proof of this lies in God's infinity. For the infinite must have limitless perfection—including the perfection of existence everywhere—and must be free from every limitation—such as being bounded or constrained within the limits of any place or places.

4. We indicate God's *immutability* when we say that God is changeless in His infinite perfection. If God could be changed, He would necessarily lose one state of being and acquire another. But God is necessary and infinite Being; He *must* be, and be as He *is;* besides, the infinite Being cannot lose or acquire anything. Therefore, with God "there is no change or shadow of alteration."

c) THE ATTRIBUTES OF GOD'S INTELLECT

God's intellect, and all His knowledge, are one with His essence. The chief attributes of God in point of knowledge or intellect are His *omniscience* and His *wisdom.*

1. We indicate God's omniscience when we say,

"God knows all things, even our most secret thoughts, words, and actions." To say that God is omniscient is to say that He is *all-knowing*. Nothing—past, present, to come, actual, possible—is absent from the perfect knowledge of God. God knows Himself perfectly, and He knows all things in and through Himself in such wise that He is not dependent upon the truth which He knows, but the truth is dependent upon Him.—The proof of these assertions lies in the fact that God is both infinite and necessary Being. If there could be anything, actual or possible, hidden from God's knowledge, then God would not be infinite; He would be limited by the limitation of His knowledge. And if God were dependent upon the truths that He knows, His knowledge would be *contingent,* and, since God's knowledge is a substantial actuality which is one with the divine essence, God himself would be *contingent* and not *necessary.*

2. We indicate God's *wisdom* when we say that God knows perfectly how best to accomplish what He wills to have done. God is all-wise. Wisdom in *creatures* (men or angels) is different from knowledge. Knowledge may consist, for creatures, in mere information; while wisdom is rather the ability to use information to best advantage. A man may *know* all the contents of all the books in all the libraries, and still be *unwise;* another man may have but little *knowledge,* but be very *wise* in his use of it. In God, however, knowledge and wisdom are one with each

other and with the divine essence, which is infinite. Hence God is *infinite wisdom.*

d) THE ATTRIBUTES OF GOD'S WILL

God's will is one with His essence. The chief attributes of God's will are *freedom, omnipotence, holiness.* In considering God's holiness (or *sanctity*) we discern the attributes of *goodness* and *mercy,* on the one hand, and of *justice* (with *veracity* and *fidelity*), on the other.

1. God, being infinite in all perfection, is perfectly *free.* Since God is the necessary and infinite *First Being,* there is no other being that can constrain Him or exact His obedience. Nor is God forced by His own nature to perform any of His acts; for self-forcing in an infinite being is a contradiction. Infinite perfection includes *perfect freedom.*

2. We indicate God's *omnipotence* when we say, "God can do all things, and nothing is hard or impossible to Him." To say that God is omnipotent is to say that He is *almighty* (i. e., all-mighty, all-powerful). God does not make any *effort* in accomplishing what He wills to do, nor is He limited to one work at a time, nor is He fatigued by His work, nor is His work built up, so to speak, bit by bit. God perfectly accomplishes what He wills to do by the eternal decrees of His perfect *will.* With God, to will and to perform is one and the same act.—The proof of these assertions is found in God's infinite perfection. In-

finite perfection includes boundless power, and excludes the imperfections of toil, effort, fatigue, successive partial accomplishment, etc.

3. We indicate God's *sanctity* or *holiness* when we say that God is all-holy. Holiness consists in the loving and willing of what is good. Now, God Himself is infinite and substantial Good. Therefore, the perfect love of God and the perfect willing of what God wills, is perfect holiness. As we have seen, God knows Himself perfectly, and thus knows Himself as all-perfect, all-good, all-lovable, and He recognizes this perfection by loving Himself perfectly. And God's will is one with Himself. Hence, God's infinite love of Himself and His infinite identity with His will constitutes God as the infinite lover and willer of what is Good, —constitutes God in infinite holiness.—This point is obvious; it needs no proof; it is reached by direct reasoning upon the infinite perfection of God.

God's sanctity or holiness shows itself in the further attributes of *goodness* and *mercy* towards His creatures, and in the perfect *justice* with which He deals with them. For: (A) God is *good* to His creatures. He creates them, preserves them, bestows boundless benefits upon them, such as life, health, great dignity (in man and angels) and a destiny to eternal happiness (men and angels). Further, God is *merciful,* for He averts many evils from His creatures, and notably from man; and God forgives penitent man the worst offences. (B) God is *just,* and His rewards and punishments are perfectly suited to merit and demerit. He is *faithful* (attribute of *fidelity*) to His promises; as, for example, to His promise of a Redeemer for man. God is also *true* (attribute of *veracity*) in all that He reveals.—The proof of all these attributes as facts in the Divine Being is founded upon the *absolutely infinite perfection* of God.

SUMMARY OF THE ARTICLE

In this Article we have learned what is meant by an *attribute* of anything, and we have studied the manner in which this term is to be applied to God's perfections, viz., *not* as if these perfections were distinct from God's essence or from one another, but in such wise that, while they are studied separately, they are understood to be really one with one another and one with the undivided and infinite essence of God.

In studying God's nature we learned the fundamental attributes of God's necessity, infinity, unity, simplicity, spirituality. In the present Article we have learned the further divine attributes of *Being* (eternity, ubiquity, immensity, immutability), of *Intellect* (knowledge and wisdom), and of *Will* (freedom, omnipotence, holiness, goodness, mercy, justice, veracity, fidelity).

In the whole Chapter on God's Nature and Attributes we have found many perfections of God that we had already discovered in the First Chapter as belonging to the First Cause. Well, our present Chapter was another angle, another approach, another view of God, whose existence was proved directly in the First Chapter, and we have had to repeat much in this direct study that was indirectly supplied to our knowledge in reasoning to and identifying the First Cause, the First Mover, the First Designer, etc.

We conclude this Chapter with a brief consideration of some difficulties that may be presented for solution to the Catholic Apologist.

1. "If God is immutable, how is He free? Is not the fact of His immutability a thing that binds Him in motionless fixity in such a way as to make free activity impossible to Him?" Not at all. Consider: God is *eternal;* all is *present* to Him; there is no flow of events or objects to which, so to speak, God needs adapt Himself taking suitable free measures. God's decrees are all *eternal,* and all perfectly *free.* Being eternal, they do not conflict with immutability. Every possible contingency in the world is eternally known to God—"foreknown" as we should say from our time-limited standpoint; and *eternal, free, immutable* decrees are made to meet every possible contingency in the most perfect manner.

2. "But God created the world *in time.* The world is not eternal. How could God create *in time* if He is fixed in an eternal immutability?" God from eternity decreed that the world should have beginning at a

point of time, or rather at the beginning of time, for
time comes into being with creation. But time cannot affect God; it is but a measure of things creatural.
God's free eternal decree to create came into realization, as freely and eternally decreed, *in time*. Or rather
God's decree to create found its realization as He
freely wished; and in being realized it brought the
thing called time with it into existence. There is
nothing in this that conflicts with either divine freedom or divine immutability.

3. "Well, if God is immutable, if He is utterly
changeless, how can my prayers make any difference?
If God's decrees are all from eternity, how can they
be affected by prayers offered in time?" God's eternal
decrees need not be affected; God has prepared, from
eternity, an answer to every prayer that can possibly
be made; and such answer is part of His eternal decrees. Of course, the prayers must be offered, else the
prepared answer cannot be given. Hence, the *necessity*
of prayer. God has revealed to us His will that we
pray; He has commanded us to pray. "Watch and
pray . . ."; "Ask and you shall receive . . .";
"Pray, therefore, brethren . . ."; "This kind is not
cast out but *by prayer* and fasting"; "If you ask the
Father anything in my name, he will give it you."
These and a hundred other texts of Holy Scripture
urge men to pray and assure them a hearing and an
answer. Still, we need not go to Scripture for a proof
of the point in question. Reason makes the matter

clear. God, the all-perfect Father of men, has implanted in the hearts of His children a longing for His gifts and a tendency to ask for them; and this would be futile on the part of God if prayer could not be *effectively* offered: and God performs no futilities, for He is all-wise. Thus, our prayers *do* make a difference, a great difference, *all* the difference! The eternal answer is waiting for every petition—but the petition must be made. The boundless gifts of God await the offering of diligent prayer—only the diligent prayer must be offered. There is no prayer that a man can offer to God that God has not known ("foreknown" as we say in our time-limited way), and for which He has failed to prepare an answer from eternity. There is no more impious remark than the flippancy, "There's no use praying; everything is fated and fixed."

4. "God is omnipotent. He can do all things. Can God, then, make a square circle? Can God make an object that shall be entirely black and also entirely white? Can God utter a truth that is false or a lie that is true?" Certainly not. God can do all things, but what you suggest are not things, but *denials of things.* You suggest contradictions, that is, two things, one of which negatives or cancels the other: the result is simply zero. A "square circle" is "a circle that is *not* a circle"; in other words, it is nothingness. Your suggestion is like this: you draw a circle on the blackboard. Then you erase it carefully, leaving not a

trace of the drawing. Then you stand back, and, pointing to empty space, you say, "Can God make that?"
Make *what?* There is nothing there!—If God could
do the unthinkable and could create contradictions as
things, He would not be all-perfect, for He would not
be all-true. To say that God cannot contradict Himself by performing contradictions is not to assert any
lack of power in God; it is to assert perfection in
God. Indeed, we all assert such a perfection when we
make an act of faith and say, "God *cannot* deceive or
be deceived." This is not the denial of omnipotence;
it is the assertion of omniscience and infinite truthfulness.

5. "God is omniscient. He knows all things. He
knows, therefore, whether I am to be saved or lost.
As He knows it, it will happen. What, therefore, is the
use of my striving to work out my salvation?" What
God knows about my ultimate fate, *I* do not know,
and *cannot* know, and it is an insane impertinence for
me to try to find out. What I *do* know is this: *I can
be saved if I will to be,* and if I carry that will into
active execution by a diligent use of God's grace. This
is a certain piece of knowledge, and it is sufficient.
Besides, God's knowledge does not affect my free-
will; it does not forestall me; it does not force me;
it does not constrain my acts. God *wants* me to save
my soul, for He "wills all men to be saved"; He gives
me every help, every grace that I require, to the end
that I may be saved. The objection here considered is

utterly foolish, utterly impertinent, and suggests a thought that is utterly false. To see it in its true character, let us consider an analogy or two—unworthy analogies, for human life is far too noble a thing to be compared to "a game" or "a business." But, notwithstanding the unworthiness of the figure, what should we think of the members of a football team that reached the following conclusion on the eve of an important game : "God knows all things. He knows whether we shall be defeated or win to-morrow. As He knows it, it will infallibly happen. What, therefore, is the use of our striving to win the game?" What should we think of a young man, embarked upon a business career with *certain* promise of success if he were industrious, who should say, "God knows all. He knows whether I shall succeed or go bankrupt. As He knows it, it will infallibly happen. What, therefore, is the use of my trying to make a success of this business?" We should regard this young man, and we should regard the members of the football team, as beneath human contempt. So must we then regard ourselves if pride, weakness, and impudence unite to lead us to make such a remark as that set down at the head of this paragraph. If tempted to make that insane remark, or to entertain the impious thought that it expresses, we should say to ourselves : "God knows, and I know, that I shall infallibly be saved *if* I am diligent in the matter of working out my salvation. God knows, and I know, that 1 *must* be saved if I avoid sin and practice the knowledge, love, and service of God, in the exercise of the true religion, as a worthy member of the true Church."

CHAPTER III

THE ACTION OF GOD UPON THE WORLD

We have seen that the world has a First Cause which *produced* it. We have seen further that the world is contingent, in other words, that it does not contain in itself the sufficient reason for its existence. Hence, the world must not only be produced, but must also be *preserved* in existence by a power outside itself. Finally, we have seen that the world is designed to serve an end; it therefore requires direction or *government* toward that end. God's action upon the world is an action of production, preservation, and government.

The present Chapter deals with these matters in three Articles, as follows:

Article 1. The Production of the World
Article 2. The Preservation of the World
Article 3. The Government of the World

ARTICLE 1. THE PRODUCTION OF THE WORLD

a) False Theories about the Production of the World
b) The Fact of Creation

a) FALSE THEORIES ABOUT THE PRODUCTION OF THE WORLD

Here we discuss *Materialism* and *Pantheism*. Materialism teaches that nothing exists but bodily being or matter, and that the world, as we see it, is but a development of an original mass of matter. Pantheism (from the Greek words *pan*, "all," and *theos*, "God") teaches that the divine substance alone exists, and that the world and all things in it are outpourings or manifestations of this substance.

1. *Materialism.*—Nothing exists but bodily matter. There is no spirit, no soul, no God. Matter is eternal and uncaused. Matter is composed of tiny particles (atoms) which have an indwelling force of motion. The motion of atoms goes on exerting itself according to changeless physical laws. As a result of this motion, the atoms are variously grouped and united, and thus different "kinds" of bodies emerge —minerals, plants, brutes, men. But there is no real diversity among these things; there is only apparent diversity, which is accounted for by atomic motion. All things in the world are as truly one in kind, and the product of an original and eternal mass of homogeneous matter, as a variety of differently shaped and differently cooked biscuits is the product of one original mass of dough.

Materialism cannot be true. If matter alone existed, then it would have to be *self-existing*. Now, as we have seen, a self-existing being must be necessary and not contingent; it must be infinite and not finite; it must be simple and not composed; it must be immutable and not full of change. But, as a fact, the world is contingent, finite, composed, and full of change. Therefore, matter cannot be self-existent, and it requires an efficient *cause* to account for its existence—a cause that is ultimately the First Cause, which is necessary, simple, infinite, and immutable. No one can doubt that the world is contingent, else it would *have* to exist, and there could be no change in it; it would have to be always just what it is unchanged and unchangeable. No one can doubt that the world is finite, for it is made up of mensurable, limited objects, and the sum of limited things is still finite and cannot be infinite. No one can question the fact that the world is composed, for the world and things in it are made up of parts. No one can deny that the world is full of change, for it is clearly in motion (as the atomists themselves assert), and is full of births, deaths, renewals, physical change, chemical change, mechanical change.

If materialism were true, then mind and matter would be the same; or rather, mind would be but a phase or development of matter. But matter always has extension; and mind has no extension. Besides, mind can deal with things that transcend the limits of matter, things like unity, truth, goodness, honor, ideals, appreciation of poetry, music, art, etc. Further, if materialism were true, there could be no accounting for intellectual knowledge or free-will. Material objects are essentially individual, and intellectual knowledge is essentially founded upon universal ideas or concepts. Free-will is self-direction following intellectual judgment, and matter is essentially inert and not self-directive.

If materialism were true, then every one of the particles of matter (atoms) would be necessary, eternal, infinite! A thing made up of parts, as matter is made up of atoms, can only amount to the sum of its parts, and if these be finite (as *parts* must be!) then the whole sum of parts is finite. Yet matter is infinite, say the materialists, for it is eternal and uncaused. Therefore, infinity must belong to each and every particle of matter. This conclusion is obviously absurd and self-contradictory. Hence materialism cannot be true.

Finally, if materialism were true, each atom of matter would be necessarily endowed with force or motion. Yet, as we have seen, motion is essentially a thing given, communicated, received. Motion is not self-originating, but must be traced to a first mover, itself unmoved. How, then, does the atom get its necessary motion? If nothing but matter exists, motion in matter becomes an utter impossibility.

For all these reasons we reject materialism as a theory wholly incapable of explaining the production of the world.

2. *Pantheism.*—There is but one substance; this is God. The world and all things in the world are either outpourings (*emanations*) of the divine substance, or *manifestations* of God. In other words, the world is to God what inlets are to the sea, what sparks are to

the fire from which they spring; or the world is a
manifestation of God as a smile is a manifestation of
mind, or as a ripple on a lake is a manifestation of a
condition affecting water, or as wind is a manifestation of atmospheric disturbance. Pantheism of the
first type is called *Emanationism;* pantheism of the
second type is called *Phenomenalism.* There is a third
type of pantheism called *Idealistic,* of which we need
only say that it is a very vague and abstract doctrine
of God as a kind of idea (called *The Absolute*) which
comes gradually out of its abstract state into concrete-
ness by realizing itself in things.

Pantheism, in whatever form presented, identifies
the world with God. This doctrine cannot be true.

Pantheism contradicts reason. Reason demonstrates the impossibility of a cause producing itself
as its own effect; yet pantheism makes the First
Cause and Necessary Being one with the world, which
is caused and contingent being. Further, pantheism
teaches a kind of evolution in God (for He emits
emanations, manifestations, or develops concrete
realization of Himself), and thus posits change in
the Necessary Being, growth in the Perfect Being,
improvement in the Infinite Being!

Pantheism contradicts consciousness. Each of us
recognizes himself as an individual being distinct
from all others. This consciousness must be altogether deceiving if pantheism be true, for then we
are nothing but emanations, manifestations, or

"parts" of God! And if consciousness so deceives us, we must not trust it at all; so we cannot be sure of anything that we perceive or reason out: hence all doctrines, including pantheism, become utterly uncertain and futile; there is nothing left but the absurd self-contradiction of universal scepticism.

Pantheism would lead to unthinkable consequences in practical life. Pantheism destroys personality in men and makes all men one with one another and one with God. Thus there can be no individual free-will, no individual responsibility. The murderer and his victim, the saint and the sinner, the patriot and the traitor, are all one, are all God! There can be no crime then, for all human action is God's action, and God cannot commit crime. Thus there is no morality, and laws and governments become futile inanities.

For these reasons we are forced to reject pantheism as a theory wholly incapable of explaining the production of the world.

Pantheism and Materialism are called *monism* (from the Greek word *monos* "one," "alone") because they teach that the universe is made of one single kind of substance, viz., either the divine substance, or matter.

b) THE FACT OF CREATION

With materialism and pantheism rejected as utterly inadequate, we are left but one doctrine on the production of the world. This doctrine, therefore, must, by exclusion, be true. It is called the doctrine of *Creationism,* and it asserts that the world was produced by an act of God's infinite will, which called it out of nothingness into real existence.

Creation is *the production out of nothing of a thing in its entirety.* It is, first of all, an act of production, of efficient causality. Further, creation is an act of efficient causality which produces *the entire effect* out of nothing. In this we notice that creation is different from all other acts of efficient production. A carpenter builds a house, but he does not create the house; his work is merely an adaptation and use of *preëxisting materials,* and there is nothing preëxistent for creation to deal with. A dressmaker may call the product of her art "a creation"; but it is obvious that her work is merely the arrangement and shaping of materials which she did not herself produce. A poet may call his latest sonnet "a creation," but the poet does not create his thoughts and fancies: they are fundamentally drawn from a material world which the senses perceive, and which the poet did not produce or help to produce. A creation is a thing produced without preëxisting materials. To create is to produce a thing, entirely and completely, out of nothing.

Now the world is a fact; it is here. In answering the question, "How did the world get here?" we must not say that it caused itself, for that would be to assert the absurdity that it existed as a cause to give itself existence as an effect. Nor can we say that the world is an outpouring, a manifestation or realization of God, as pantheism teaches. Nor can we say that the world is eternal, uncaused, infinite, and necessary, as materialism asserts. There is only one answer left: *the world was created.* And thus, even now, we may say that the fact of creation stands proved by exclusion.

We offer also one direct or positive proof of the fact of creation. Whatever is found in a thing belongs to that thing of necessity, or is shared to that thing by another in which it is found of necessity. Thus if a piece of iron is hot, we know that, since iron is not of necessity hot, heat was communicated to the iron by that which is, of its nature, hot, viz., fire. Now, existence belongs of necessity only to that being which must exist and cannot be non-existent; in a word, existence belongs of necessity to God alone. Therefore, when other things are found in possession of existence, it follows that existence was communicated to them by that which has existence of necessity, i. e., by God. That is to say, the chain of communicated existences in things must *ultimately* lead to God, the First and Necessary Cause. Hence, existence in the world points to God as the Cause, the Producer of the world. Now, how did God produce the world? Not out of His own substance, for He is infinite and immutable. Not out of some other substance, for no substance exists which has not its exist-

ence from God, and if we say that God made the
world out of a pre-existing substance, our question
merely shifts to this substance, and we ask, "How did
God produce *that?*" Ultimately, we must reach the
conclusion that God made substances out of no pre-
existing substances at all. In other words, God made
substances out of nothing, that is to say, He *created*
substances. And whether the world were developed
out of other substances into its present form, or was
made just as we behold it, in any case the ultimate answer to the question of the world's production is this:
The world was created.

In Scripture we read that God made the world in
six days. The Hebrew word "yom" is rendered by
"day" in the English translation of the Bible. But
"yom" really means a period of undetermined length.
It matters not whether God willed (from eternity)
that the world should develop slowly or quickly into
its present form. In any case, there were six periods or
stages of development in the work. This does not
mean that the world "evolved" or that it did not; it
merely means that six definite stages of creation are
a revealed truth. We add, in passing, that it also
means that man's creation was a separate and distinct
creation—a special act by which God breathed upon
the face of man and man became a living soul.

The six days of creation are not solar or sun days,
for the sun was not made until the fourth day of crea-

tion. Whether they were long or short periods we do not know. Experimental science seems to indicate that they were long, very long. Time, however, has nothing to do with the fact. Time, indeed, comes into existence with creatures, and is a measure affecting creatures only, and not God. The six days of creation are known as the *Hexahemeron,* a word derived from the Greek *hex,* "six," and *hemera,* "day."

God freely chooses to create, for, since He is all-perfect, He is utterly free and in no wise necessitated in His acts. God is not moved or motivated to create. Hence God has no *motive,* in the strict sense of that term. Still, God has an end and purpose in creating, for He is most wise, and to act without purpose would be to act unwisely. Hence, we rightly say that God has a purpose, an end in view, in creating, but that He is not stirred to create by any motive.

Now God cannot have made creatures for them-selves; creatures are utterly contingent and cannot be an end in themselves; they have nothing of being, nothing of value, to serve as an end except what God gives them. It must be, then, that God, in creating, acts *toward Himself* as toward an end. Hence God is not only the First Efficient Cause of creatures; He is also the Last End or Final Cause for which creatures exist. Theologians prove the truth that God creates for *His external formal and objective glory.* In a word, God creates for Himself as the only end worthy of divine action.

In this bodily world the chief of creatures (i. e., of things created) is man. Man alone of worldly creatures has a spiritual and immortal soul and a free will. Other creatures exist to help man maintain life and to achieve a measure of happiness here; they exist to help man to live his life on earth in a manner suitable to win him happiness for eternity. That man has a spiritual and immortal soul and free-will is proved in Rational Psychology, a department of Philosophy. Apologetics can give but the briefest of arguments— albeit the arguments are incontrovertible—for the existence of a spiritual and immortal soul and free-will in man.

1. *Man has a spiritual soul.* That which exercises spiritual (i. e., real but non-material) functions is itself spiritual, for the action of a thing manifests its nature, and no effect can exceed its cause in excellence or perfection. Now the soul of man exercises spiritual functions. The soul thinks, reflects, reasons, is aware of such non-material things as beauty, goodness, truth, unity, honor, glory, ideals. It has self-consciousness by which it can perfectly *bend back* or *reflect* upon itself—a thing which no material or bodily thing can do : the eye does not see itself seeing, the ear does not hear itself hearing, but the soul can think of itself thinking, can know itself knowing, can make itself and its acts the object of its own study and inquiry. Therefore the soul, since it exercises spiritual functions, is itself spiritual.

2. *Man has an immortal soul.* Whatever is spiritual is *simple,* i. e., not made up of physical parts. Such parts are essentially the component elements of *material* things. Now the soul of man is spiritual; hence it is not made up of parts. But whatever is not made up of parts cannot be separated into parts. And whatever cannot be separated into parts cannot die—for death is precisely the breaking up of a living thing into its essential physical parts. Therefore, man's soul cannot die. In other words, it is immortal.

3. *Man has free-will.* Man is possessed of an indestructible conviction that he is the author of his own acts, and that he has freely chosen to do what he has done, but could have done otherwise. Man is inevitably conscious of his own proper responsibility for what he does: he reproaches himself for having done some things, he approves of his conduct in other instances. If this consciousness be deceiving, there is no truth to be had by human means at all, and there is no certainty in anything, no learning, no science. Again, if man be not free in his choice of individual human acts, then all laws, governments, courts, are absurdities. All human law is based upon the obvious fact of man's freedom: laws are made *to direct free choice* lest it be hurtfully abused. Laws are not made for houses or trees or horses, but *for man;* for only the agent that can break a law is free to keep a law. The conviction of man's freedom is as obvious

and universal as the conviction of the world's existence. Deny this conviction, and you deny all validity in human knowledge. Man, therefore, has free-will.

Since man alone of all worldly creatures has the surpassing excellences of a spiritual and immortal soul and free-will, man is the most perfect, the chief, the most important, of creatures in this world.

SUMMARY OF THE ARTICLE

In this Article we have studied the three doctrines advanced to account for the production of the world, viz., Materialism, Pantheism, and Creationism. We have seen that the first two doctrines are necessarily to be rejected as involving contradictions and as leading to practical consequences of unthinkable character. Creationism being thus proved by exclusion, we have studied it directly and have advanced positive proof of its truth. We have looked briefly at the Biblical account of creation in the *Hexahemeron,* or six days of creation, and have noticed that man is a special creation of God. We have seen that God is perfectly free in creating, not being moved to create, but choosing to create for the only worthy end, which is Himself. Finally, we have declared that man is the chief of worldly creatures, and have established the claim by proving man possessed of a spiritual and immortal soul and free-will.

ARTICLE 2. THE PRESERVATION OF THE WORLD

a) Meaning of Preservation   b) The Fact of Preservation

a) MEANING OF *PRESERVATION*

We have already used the word *creature* many times. A creature is a created thing. It is anything real that is not God. The world and all things in it are creatures. Creatures, not being God, are contingent; they depend for their production upon their causes and ultimately upon the First Efficient Cause, which is God. Now, the dependence of creatures not only affects their production, the *origin* of their existence; it also affects the *maintenance* of their existence. Creatures have not in themselves a sufficient reason for their existence, and this is true of *every moment* of that existence, and not only of the moment when they *begin* to exist. The maintenance of creatures in existence is what we mean by the preservation of the world.

The existence of all creatures depends upon God, the Creator and Preserver, in such a way that they could not last even for a moment, but would lapse into nothingness if the divine power did not hold them in existence. This exercise of God's power we call *Preservation* or *Conservation*.

We use the word *preservation* in several different but related senses. We speak of preserving health, of preserving virtue, of preserving foodstuffs. In these expressions we refer to the influence that creatures may exercise one upon another. Thus health (a creature) is preserved by the creatures called proper food, clothing, shelter, light, air, exercise, etc. Thus virtue (a creature) is preserved by the creatures called striving after good, avoidance of evil, use of grace, prayer, watchfulness, etc. Thus the creatures called foodstuffs are preserved by the creatures called fire (in cooking), salt, ice, etc. In our present study, however, we speak of preservation *in existence,* and we say that things in the world are preserved in existence even when they undergo continual accidental and substantial changes. We speak of that preservation which keeps creatures from *annihilation* or reduction to nothingness. If foodstuffs be not preserved, they decay; but they are not annihilated; they are preserved as existent things, even if they are no longer suitable for use as food. Therefore, the fact of accidental and substantial change in bodily creatures does not affect our acceptance of the term *preservation.* In reference to bodies, preservation means that no quantity of matter perishes—a truth which physical science establishes. In reference to spirits (souls of men) we mean that they continue in existence without substantial change.

b) THE FACT OF PRESERVATION

As an infinite power is required to give existence (create), so the same power is required to preserve creatures to whom existence has been given. The proof of this assertion lies in the fact that creatures, in origin and continuance, are essentially dependent upon the First Cause. We state the proof in two ways:

1. The dependence of the world (of all creatures) on the Creator is an *essential* dependence. It is like the dependence of heat upon fire, of daylight upon the sun; it is not like the dependence of a statue upon the sculptor who made it. If heat is to be maintained, the fire must be kept up. If daylight is not to cease, the sun must not disappear. A statue may endure a thousand years after its sculptor is dead; but the sculptor only gave the statue *accidental* being, inasmuch as he merely shaped and arranged a thing which had its existence as a thing independently of him, and the shaping inheres in that thing. We repeat: the dependence of the world on the Creator is an *essential,* not an *accidental,* dependence. Now, an essential dependence means that the very essence of the dependent thing must cease if the active force upon which the thing depends ceases to be exercised. Thus the essence of the world must cease to exist if its dependence upon the Creator be not maintained. In other words, unless *preserved* by the power that gave it existence, the world must lapse into non-existence. Hence, preservation of the world is a fact.

2. The Creator freely chooses to give the world existence. But existence is not a thing that the world can take and keep of itself; for, after creation, it

would then be self-existent; and self-existence requires an infinite subject and the world is finite. Hence, God, freely choosing to give the world existence, must freely choose to continue to give existence, else existence must cease. God's free choice to maintain the world in existence is *preservation* or *conservation*. The very fact that the world is here is proof that it is *maintained* here. Hence, preservation is a fact.

The dependence of the world upon the infinite power of God is like the dependence of a stone which a boy holds suspended upon a cord. The boy may will to hold the stone clear of the ground; he may hold it up for a long time; but the stone never becomes capable of sustaining itself in the air, no matter how long it is held. The moment the boy chooses to let go the cord, the stone falls to the ground. Similarly, the world is held out of nothingness by the power of the Creator, and it can remain out of nothingness only so long as the Creator freely chooses to hold it there.

As a fact, God, being infinitely wise, does not create in order utterly to destroy. He does not annihilate His creatures. But the point for recognition and remembrance here is this: the world and all creatures, bodily and spiritual, would inevitably lapse into nothingness if God did not maintain them continuously in existence.

In this very brief Article we have defined *preservation* or *conservation* as an act by which God holds the created world out of nothingness, maintains it in existence, positively acts to keep it from annihilation. We have proved the fact that the continuance of contingent things in existence requires the action of the Necessary Being.

The fact of divine preservation ought to stir us to admiration for the wondrous power of God, and to humble thankfulness and love toward Him who has such a care of us that He does not forget or neglect us for a single instant—no, not even when we turn against Him and insult Him by sin!

ARTICLE 3. THE GOVERNMENT OF THE WORLD

a) Meaning of World Government   b) The Fact of Divine Providence

a) MEANING OF WORLD GOVERNMENT

We have seen that God, in creating and preserving the world, has an end in view, a purpose to be attained. Being supremely wise, God cannot act without such an end. Hence, things created are *directed* toward the attainment of their end. God, creating all things for an end, must eternally decree the manner in which creatures shall attain unto that end.

In other words, God must have established a plan of *government* by which creatures are directed toward the attainment of their end.

Creatures, then, are governed unto the achievement of their end. But we have two kinds of creatures in the world, viz., the free, and those destitute of freedom. Man has free choice; other worldly creatures have not. Hence the eternal decrees by which God governs the world must be suited to the natures that he has made. The creatures that have no freedom will be governed by *necessity,* that is, without choice, or possibility of refusal of obedience. Thus minerals, plants, and brute animals are governed by *physical laws.* Man, who has free choice, has understanding by which he is aware of an order in things that he is called upon to observe and forbidden to disturb; but man is not necessitated; in his free acts he is guided by *suasion,* but is not forced. Man as a body is subject to physical laws, like the law of gravitation and the law of inertia; as an animal, he is subject to the physical laws of nutrition, growth, etc.; but as a rational free creature, he is subject to the moral law as recognized by reason (conscience), and this law is called *the natural law.* Thus, creatures are governed by *physical laws* and by *the natural law.* Man alone, among worldly creatures, is subject to the natural law.

The natural law is a moral law; it is not a physical

law; it does not *enforce* obedience, but invites it and shows it reasonable and right. Can man, then, refuse to obey the natural law? Certainly he can. Does man, by such disobedience, thwart the plans of God and render the end of creation unattainable? No, for the end of creation will infallibly be attained. We have seen that this end is the external glory of God; and if man does not show forth this glory in Heaven, he will manifest it by showing the divine justice in hell. But man may indeed fail to attain his end inasmuch as it affects himself. God wants man to attain to eternal happiness in the possession of Himself; and man, if he is to attain this end, must freely choose to attain it. Now man is prone to evil, to sin, and, unless God had prepared special helps for him, he would surely fail to attain his last end. But the all-perfect Creator and Preserver of the world is also its all-perfect Governor; and God has *provided* for all contingencies, and has arranged from eternity all requisite helps and graces that will enable man to choose well and choose effectively in the attainment of his last end. And the whole government of the world by physical laws, by the natural law, and by the law of special helps (or law of grace) belongs to what we call the *Providence of God*.

God *governs* the world. The fact of physical law and the natural law manifests this truth to us. We may say that God's government of the world is the expression of His *providence*.

b) THE FACT OF DIVINE PROVIDENCE

In proving the existence of God we used the Argument from Design and directed attention to the marvellous order observable in the world. Now, order is neither more nor less than a suitable arrangement of means for the attainment of a foreseen and intended end. Thus order is inevitably the expression of plan and purpose. In a word, order in the world is the physical expression of the world's *government* according to the *providence* of God.

If we deny the existence of Divine Providence (and its expression in the government of the world) we must make this denial for one of three reasons, viz., (1) God does not know how to rule the world to the extent of providing for the fulfilment of His end even in smallest details, acts, movements, events; or (2) God does not have the power so to rule the world; or (3) God has no care, no concern about the world, and it is a matter of indifference to Him whether the world attains or fails to attain its end. These reasons are not admissible. The first makes God imperfect in point of knowledge; the second, in point of power; the third, in point of wisdom. But, as we have seen, God is all-knowing, all-powerful, all-wise, as He is infinitely perfect. Therefore, once the fact of God's infinite perfection is admitted, the fact of His providence must also be acknowledged.

Those who deny Divine Providence are, above others, Materialists, Pantheists, Fatalists, Deists,

Casualists. Pantheists and Materialists are forced by their strange doctrine on the production of the world to deny providence in the world; but we have seen that this doctrine is false and absurd. Fatalists assert that some blind cosmic force is at the back of things and causes all acts and events to occur precisely as they do occur; but this doctrine contradicts common sense and experience, involves the denial of free-will, and denies the Divine Intelligence and Will, making them a blind and meaningless force. Deists say that God has made the world, but has ceased to care for it, and has tossed it aside as a child tosses a toy of which it has grown tired; but this doctrine contradicts *preservation,* which we have seen to be a fact (Chap. III, Art. 2), and denies the Divine Wisdom, for certainly it would be unwise in the Creator to make the world for an end, and then to care nothing whether that end were attained. Casualists teach that the acts and events of the world are the outcome of sheer chance (Latin *casus,* "chance") ; but we have seen the futility of the chance theory (Chap. I, Art. 3, a). We perceive, then, that the doctrines opposed to the facts of Divine Providence are unworthy of attention, and are flatly inadmissible.

The most notable reason urged against the fact of Divine Providence is the existence of physical and moral evil in the world. We have considered this difficulty in another place (Chap. I, Art. 3, c), but.

there is need for direct and particular study of the matter here.

1. *Physical Evil.*—Physical evil is that which affects the nature or activities of things. Common examples of such evil are: sickness, death, pain, lameness, wounds, deformities, debility, poverty, plagues, famine, results of wars, etc. Physical evil is alleged as an argument against Divine Providence by those who say: "How can an all-good and all-powerful God permit His children to be afflicted by such hardships, such woes, such miseries?" We answer: There would be value in the complaint if: (i) God's end in creation were thwarted by the existence of physical evil, or (ii) the existence of physical evil conflicted with the perfection of God. But neither condition is verified. For:

(i) Physical evils do not thwart the end of creation. The end of creation is the glory of God and the eternal happiness of men. Now, physical evils are often a help to man, and not a hindrance, in the task of working out his salvation. Sickness, poverty, pain, and other physical ills have often turned the minds of men away from the pursuit of fleeting things and fixed their purpose upon eternal verities and values. These ills or evils are an evidence to man that he is not as God made him, but is of a race that has suffered a loss and has been injured by a Fall. And, while physical evils may be justly regarded

as punishments for sin, as deprivations effected by
the primal sin of humanity, they may also be regarded, with greater justice, as mercies and kindnesses. Do we not need continual prods to remind
us that we have not our be-all and end-all in health
or wealth or worldly success or fame or a career?
Is it not a merciful dispensation that tends to make
us see life as it is, against the light and the background of eternity? Is it not a kindness that makes
us see, in however much tribulation and sorrow, that
this world is not our final home, but our workshop;
not our field of victory, but our field of battle? Besides, life is not all misery; life is not a continuous
scourge of physical evil. Indeed, life presents so much
that is attractive and joy-giving that men are strongly
inclined to live it for these things, and, without physical evils to afflict them, they would inevitably run into
excess and inordinateness, and so fail of attaining
their last end. When we come to the question of just
why such and such evils afflict such and such men,
we cannot, of course, make answer. The thing is a
mystery. We must simply trust God, who gives us
a thousand evidences of His love and care for one
evil that He allows to afflict us. We must know, from
the thousand evident expressions of care, that there
is reason for the affliction, or it simply would not be.
And what is our own love toward God worth—protest it how we may—if it cannot endure obscurity
in the inscrutable designs of providence, and if it

cannot bear the occasional evils that come to us, and evils of which God is not the author?—Some men complain of *injustice* when they are made to suffer evils, especially when they feel that they suffer more than other men. This complaint is simply insanity. None of us has a claim in justice to life; God is not bound to give us anything. And the gifts He does give us, life and reason and free-will, are so great and wonderful that we are fools indeed to complain of any conditions under which they are received or held. To complain that we are not treated fairly in life, is to make a complaint as silly as that of the man who received a wholly unmerited gift of one million dollars, and then complained because one of the bills was a little soiled. Chesterton (*Orthodoxy,* pp. 101 f.) says: "If the miller's third son said to the fairy, 'Explain why I must not stand on my head in the fairy palace,' the other might fairly reply, 'Well, if it comes to that, explain the fairy palace.' If Cinderella says, 'How is it that I must leave the ball at twelve?' her godmother might answer, 'How is it that you are going there till twelve?' " So when weak human beings complain, "How is it that I must suffer these ills in my life?" we may reasonably answer, "How is it that you enjoy this glorious life?" If the weakling whines, "Explain why I am made to live in misery," we may fairly answer, "Explain why you are allowed to live at all." If life were only for this world and for time, then physical

evils would be unmixed hardships; but since life is
what it is, a brief but glorious *opportunity* for un-
told glory and unending happiness, then evils which
make us, or tend to make us, realize life's purpose are
not unmixed hardships, but kindnesses and blessings.
And it is God and God's providence that turns physical evils to man's account and makes them blessings
in disguise; for God is not the author of such evils;
they come from creatures, and all of them have their
roots in that first bad choice of free man that wrecked
the world. Hence, far from being an argument against
providence, physical evils are actually an evidence of
God's loving providence for His creatures.

(ii) Physical evils are not an evidence of imperfection in God. We have already seen the proof of
this in our discussion of the first point. Physical evils
are not of God's authorship, and they are turned by
God to man's account. In this we have evidence of
God's perfection, not of imperfection. As a sick man
is sometimes made to take bitter medicine or undergo
a painful operation to save his life, and these hardships are no evidence of unwisdom in the physician
or surgeon, but proofs of the doctor's skill, so the
physical ills which may make man, sick and wounded
by original sin, sound and strong in spiritual health,
are no evidence of unwisdom in the Divine Physician, but evidence of His wondrous skill. As a wise
and devoted father may allow his beloved son to feel
the consequences of an act of folly, in order that wis-

dom may come through bitter experience, so the most wise and loving Father of men may allow His children to suffer physical evil (although He is not the cause or author of such evil), in order that they may learn to withdraw their hopes and their trust from things of time and to fix them upon eternal values. We are forced by reason to the conclusion that the existence of physical evils is no argument against Divine Perfection, but, on the contrary, is a proof of such perfection.

2. *Moral Evil.*—Moral evil is sin, and man is its author. Sin comes from the abuse of free-will, that great gift which God gave and will not take away. God is in no sense the cause of sin. God made man free, and if He should take away freedom, He would destroy human nature. God will not contradict Himself by taking away what He gave, even if the gift be abused.

The existence of moral evil does not conflict with the wisdom of God. Nay, as in the case of physical evil, the fact of moral evil is the occasion for the manifestation of God's wisdom, power, and providence. For God often draws good out of moral evil. Consider: the persecutors of the early Christians committed horrible sins; these sins were not of God's willing, but were against His will. Abuse of freedom in man caused these sins. Yet out of them God drew the glorious fortitude of the martyrs. Again: Judas committed a crime unspeakable and terrible in the sight of God; but was not a world redeemed in consequence? God never wills moral evil—the thought is itself a blasphemy, for sin is sin precisely because it is in conflict with the Eternal Reason and Will of God. But God permits moral evil because He does not thwart free-will. God, hating sin as only infinite perfection can hate it, yet shows His marvellous power and providence by turning the very fact of sin to man's account. Thus, far from being an argument against Providence, the fact of moral evil, and the turning of its outcome to man's account, is an evidence of an all-wise Providence.

SUMMARY OF THE ARTICLE

In this Article we have studied the fact of the government of the world. We have seen in the existence of this government the expression of God's providence, which guides all things toward the ultimate end of creation. We have studied the fact of providence directly, supplying a negative argument by showing the futility and inadequacy of doctrines opposed to it. We have rounded out our proof by considering the unreasonableness of the complaint made against providence on the score of the existence of physical and moral evil.

BOOK SECOND

RELIGION

This Book takes up the first truth implied in the Existence of God, proved in Book First, viz., the existence of a relation, a bond, between God and man, a bond that is rightly recognized by man in the practice of the true religion. In this Book the nature of religion is studied, and the need of a supernatural revelation for the true and sufficient religion is indicated. The Book is divided into two Chapters, as follows:

Chapter I. The Nature of Religion
Chapter II. The Need of Revelation in Religion

THE NATURE OF RELIGION

God exists. He is the Creator, Preserver, and Ruler of all creatures. The chief of worldly creatures is man. Man has understanding and free-will, and these splendid faculties find their highest and noblest use in knowing, loving, and serving God. In such function of intellect and will man exercises the virtue of *religion*.

This Chapter deals with the nature of religion, defining it, describing it as a thing required by rational man, and as a thing found among all men of all times. The Chapter also refutes false notions that have been advanced to explain the origin of religion among men.

All these matters are dealt with in the following Articles:

Article 1. The Meaning of Religion
Article 2. The Necessity and Universality of Religion
Article 3. The Origin of Religion

Article 1. The Meaning of Religion

a) Definition   b) Division

a) DEFINITION OF *RELIGION*

To define a term by analyzing its etymology is to give a *nominal* definition; to define a term by indicating the essence for which the term stands is to give a *real* definition. A nominal definition explains the term as a *name;* a real definition explains the *thing* which is known by the name. We shall investigate both the nominal and the real import of the term *religion*.

1. *Nominal Definition.*—The term *religion* is variously derived. Cicero says it comes from *relegere*, which means "to exercise careful attention," and asserts that those who conducted public worship of the gods were carefully attentive to the usual ceremonies, and were called, in consequence, *religiosi*. Lactantius, a renowned Father of the Church who lived in the late 3rd and early 4th centuries, derives the word *religion* from the Latin *religare* "to bind," and says that it indicates the bond of duty whereby man is bound to God. St. Augustine first believed that the term *religion* is derived from *reeligere*, a Latin verb meaning "to choose again," and said that as man had lost God by sin, so by religion he sought to find or choose Him again. Later, however, St. Augustine changed his mind about this derivation and adopted that proposed by Lactantius.

2. *Real Definition.*—St. Thomas Aquinas, discussing the disagreement of authorities about the derivation of the term *religion*, says: "Whatever be the truth about the origin of the name, religion as a reality indicates the relationship of man towards God." Amplifying this definition, we may define religion as the sum-total of man's relations (duties) toward God.

Looking at religion *objectively*, or as *a thing*, we

define it as "a system of truths, laws, and practices which man recognizes and observes in paying worship to God." Viewing religion *subjectively,* i. e., as resident in the person, the *subject,* who exercises its acts, we define it as "the virtue which inclines man to render to God the honor, love, and worship, which is His due."

b) DIVISION OF RELIGION

The most important division of religion is that which classifies it as *natural* and *supernatural.*

1. Natural religion is the sum-total of man's duties to God (including truths to be known, laws and practices to be observed), inasmuch as these may be known by the natural power of human reason alone, unaided by revelation.

2. Supernatural religion is the sum-total of man's duties to God as known by divine revelation.

Man may know many of the truths of religion by his unaided reason. He may know the existence of God, and may reason out the knowledge that God is one, necessary, infinite, etc. He may also reason out the truth that man depends utterly upon God, and that the meaning of life is the knowledge, love, and service of God. But there are other truths which man's unaided reason could never know, such, for instance, as the Incarnation and the Blessed Trinity. To know these truths man must have revelation.

Now, many of the truths that man could know by

unaided reason—truths, that is to say, of the *natural religion*—are also divinely revealed. Such truths are natural in themselves, but supernatural in the manner (or *form,* as the expression is) of their manifestation. Other truths, such as the Trinity, are supernatural in themselves, being above the unaided reach of reason, and also in their manner or form, for they are divinely revealed. Truths of religion that are supernatural both in themselves and in their form, constitute *revealed religion,* strictly so called. Revealed religion is also called *positive* religion, since its truths are manifested by the positive word of God in revelation.

Supernatural truths are always found in harmony with naturally knowable truths. For truth cannot contradict truth. Reason may often find evidence to approve and manifest the truth of strictly supernatural and revealed facts *after revelation has given the first knowledge of them.* But in no case can reason find a contradiction in supernatural truths. Even the bitter enemies of God's Church, who have tried in all ways and in every age to throw discredit upon such revealed truths, have been forced to the admission that no inherent contradiction or absurdity can be shown in them.

While human reason accepts revealed or positive truths on the authority of God who reveals them, this acceptance is not blind. Human reason can know for certain that God exists, that God is all-truthful, that

God has spoken. Hence it is a requirement of reason that unshaken faith be reposed in what the all-true declares as a fact. Faith is not to be rationalized, and faith is ever a submission to God's authority; it has been well called "a genuflection of the will." But faith is always reasonable, and never unworthy of rational man. On the contrary, faith elevates and perfects the rational powers of man.

SUMMARY OF THE ARTICLE

In this very short Article we have defined religion. We have found that it is the sum-total of man's duties to God. We have looked at these duties in themselves or *objectively,* and have defined religion as the sum of truths, laws, and practices which man recognizes and observes in paying worship to God. We have looked at these duties as they exist in man, the subject of religion, and have defined religion *subjectively* as the virtue which inclines man to render to God the honor, love, and worship which is His due. Throughout our enquiry we have been thoroughly rational; we have injected no sentiment into the subject. Hence we see that religion is not a mass of tender emotions or sentiments, as most men to-day regard it. The Catholic apologist should be instant in fighting the paralyzing notion that religion is merely something tender and appealing to the feelings; for it is as cold and hard a fact as man can face, and the apologist should see to it that the men of his acquaintance really face it.—We concluded the Article by distinguishing religion as natural and supernatural.

ARTICLE 2. THE NECESSITY AND UNIVERSALITY OF RELIGION

a) The Necessity of Religion   b) The Universality of Religion

a) THE NECESSITY OF RELIGION

We speak here of religion in general, and we say that there is an obligation incumbent upon man, as a rational creature, of professing and practising religion.

Man knows by the natural light of reason that justice is to be done. Justice requires that everyone be given his due. Certainly, then, honor is due to excellence, obedience is due to just authority, love is due to that which is good and splendid and lovable, gratitude is due to the giver of great gifts. Now God, as we have seen, is infinite; hence He is perfect excellence, and honor is due Him; God is the supreme and perfect ruler of the world and of men, and therefore He is to be obeyed; God is all-perfect and therefore all-lovable, and love is His due; God is the giver of life and of all good gifts, and therefore He is to be thanked. Therefore, the highest honor, obedience, love, and gratitude are due to God; they are owed to God; justice requires that they be paid to God. But this is only saying that God is to be worshipped; or, in other words, that man has the duty of worshipping God. In a word, man must practise religion.

Thus religion is *a duty* to be rendered to God; it rests upon man as an obligation of his nature. It is not merely something to satisfy tender sensibilities or emotions; nor is it a matter of utility to man, as contributing to his earthly peace, prosperity, security, and comfort. It is a matter of plain justice, and a man who will not accept, recognize, and practise religion, is a debtor who will not pay his debts.

Religion is necessary to man, not only because *reason* requires it; it is necessary because *the whole man* requires it. The mind craves perfect truth; God is perfect truth, and man cannot attain to God without religion. The will wants to choose perfect goodness; God is perfect goodness, and man cannot achieve God without religion. The whole of human nature craves happiness in the possession of boundless good; God is the boundless good which cannot be possessed without religion.

Religion is necessary if men are to regard one another as brothers, not in mere name or sentiment—as in the cant of the day, and in the gospel of certain shoulder-slapping organizations which tend to reduce brotherhood to mere boisterousness and protestation —but in sober truth. Without the clear recognition of a common Father men shall vainly talk of human brotherhood; but the common Father is not recognized truly and actively unless He be recognized in religion.—Again, religion is necessary if the onerous duties of family life are to be recognized and fulfilled by parents; only the firm faith in a God who will reward or punish for earthly conduct will sustain husband and wife in constant union and mutual love while they fulfil the tremendously burdensome duties of rearing children, loving them, educating them, laboring for them.—Further, without religion there is no basis for respect for law or for any civil authority. For the exercise of *any* authority is always a religious act. It is a tacit appeal to a higher (and ultimately to the highest) authority, who has set or approved the ruler in his place and will back him up in it. The idea of authority always involves the idea of God—yes, even the idea of the authority of tyrants.

Religion is the necessary basis of morality. Morality consists in the relation which exists between free human activity, on the one hand, and the Eternal Law (i. e., Divine Reason and Will) or, in a word, God Himself, on the other. Hence, morality itself is religious; its norm is the line within which man must keep to make his actions carry him toward his last end; and this last end is God. Take away God, and the duty man owes to God in religion, and the line or norm of morality is removed. Conscience alone does not suffice for the enduring of morality among men; for conscience has power only when its dictates are recognized as reflecting the law of the Supreme Lawgiver. Take away the recognition of this Lawgiver from the conscience of men, and you take away all authority from conscience; without religion there is no force or validity in the dictates of conscience.

Religion, then, is necessary to men on the score of their rational nature. It is a requirement of individual man and of society.

Religion being a necessary duty, it follows that it must have its proper expression. Now, the expression of religion takes the form of *worship,* or, more accurately, *divine worship.* This worship is defined as the sum of all the acts (interior and external) by which man shows to God the honor and homage that is His due. The chief acts of worship are: (*a*) Devotion, or readiness of will and affection to elicit acts that belong to the service and praise of God; (*b*) Prayer, or the elevation of the mind to God for the purpose of adoring and praising Him, asking His pardon for offences committed against Him, imploring His aid and His gifts, and thanking Him for favors bestowed; (*c*) External adoration, or the outer manifestation of man's subjection to the divine excellence; (*d*) Sacrifice, or the external, ceremonious, and official offering to God of an object which is destroyed (really or equivalently) to manifest God's supreme dominion over all creatures, and to express man's recognition of his utter dependence upon God.

Religion is necessary to man. But religion is a thing
which requires internal and external expression, and
it is incumbent upon men both as individuals and in
society. Hence, subjective religion alone does not suffice; there must be objective religion. Now, objective religion is a system of truths, laws, and practices which regulate divine worship. Now, what if
there be several or many systems of doctrine, regula-
tions, and practices? Then, certainly, man requires
that system which is indeed a system of *truths,* justly
established laws, and authoritatively prescribed practices. In a word man requires *the true religion.*

Our whole argument in this present Article is in
evidence of the falsity of *absolute indifferentism,*
which makes religion a matter of no importance (a
matter of *indifference*) to man, and teaches that man
need practise no religion at all. Our last remark was
directed against the *qualified indifferentism* which
admits that religion is necessary, but asserts the sufficiency of any form of religion whatever. For, even
here, while speaking of religion in general, it is necessary for completeness to insert the evident statement
that man is bound to discover and to practise the
true religion. We must, however, defer detailed discussion and proof of this point to a later Chapter.

b) THE UNIVERSALITY OF RELIGION

In speaking of the *universality* of religion, or in
calling religion *universal,* we mean that religion has

existed among all men at all times. That is to say, religion *of some kind*—of some degree of perfection as the recognition of a power above the world, regulating the world and requiring the recognition of men —has always and everywhere existed. Even false religions, barbarous and monstrous religions, are a proof of this fact; for such religions are evidence that there was present in the minds and hearts of men some *notion of divinity,* some dim groping after the truth about God.

The universality of religion is attested by history, and no historical fact is more certain. Plutarch truly testifies: "No one ever saw a city without gods and temples." And Cicero declares that "Nature herself teacheth us that God is to be venerated, and of her law in this matter no man is free." Some men (like Sir John Lubbock, Baron Avebury, 1834–1913) have tried to find evidence for the existence of tribes and peoples without the idea of divinity and the sense of obligation to practise religion. Their investigations have only proved the universality of religion; and instances adduced with all confidence to prove that there have been peoples without God or gods, have in every case been disproved, and often turned the other way about. Professor C. H. Toy of Harvard (cf. *Introduction to the History of Religions,* pp. 5 f) says: "As far as our present knowledge goes, religion appears to be universal among men. There is no community of which we can say with certainty that it is without religion." Professor Tiele in his *History of Religion* declares that no tribe or nation has yet been found without a belief in some divinity; and he adds that travellers who assert the existence of such peoples have later been refuted by facts. Truly has Cicero said: "No race is so uncultured, no nation so inane, as to have minds unimbued with the notion of divinity."

We may bring to the testimony of learned men the following facts in proof of our present point: (*a*) Philology, which traces the roots of languages, gives evidence that the most important groups of languages have not only a name for God, but the *same* name. And all languages have names expressing superior powers, divinity or divinities. (*b*) Archæology, the science of antiquities, indicates the universal belief of man in a life to come, in a world superior to this, and in the company of beings superior to men, i. e., divinities. (*c*) Reason teaches us that religion is necessary to man, and that this necessity is founded in man's nature as man. We have seen this in the first section of the present Article. Now, what is required by man's nature is required by all men of all times; for human nature is not changing and variable, but remains ever the same.

SUMMARY OF THE ARTICLE

In this Article we have shown that religion is necessary to man, is a matter of obligation rooted in man's

very nature. We have seen that religion is required *by
individual man* to satisfy the craving of his heart,
the tendency of his will, the requirements of his reason, the connatural bent of the whole man. Further,
we have seen that religion is required *by human society* as the basis of true brotherhood, of justice
among men, of respect for law and authority, of the
integrity and sanctity of the family, and of all morality. We have briefly discussed the expression of religion in divine worship, and have indicated the obligation of men to express *the true religion* in their
doctrine and worship. We have drawn attention to
the falsity of religious indifferentism. We have made
a short but direct study of the universality of religion,
and have shown by historical authority, by philology,
by archæology, and by reason that religion is found
among all men of all times.

Article 3. The Origin of Religion

a) The True Origin of Religion   b) False Theories about
the Origin of Religion

a) the true origin of religion

Leaving the testimony of Holy Scripture momen-
tarily out of account, we declare that religion takes
its origin *in man's reason,* which shows him that the
world did not make itself, but must have a maker, and
ultimately a maker who is the First Cause, infinite,
necessary, all-perfect, all-powerful Being. Thus is the

existence of God made manifest to reason. Now, once the existence of the all-perfect God is known, reason further manifests the fact that man depends utterly upon God; that God is to be recognized as the First Efficient Cause and Last Final Cause of man's existence; that man must, therefore, know, love, and serve God. In a word, reason makes manifest the fundamental truths of *religion*. Therefore, the origin of religion is found in man's reason deducing truth from the consideration of the created world.

But we must not leave Holy Scripture out of account. We have not yet proved Scripture as the Word of God, nor even as a reliable historical document. It will be our task to make such a proof later. Here let us assume the fact that Scripture is reliable history. Now Scripture informs us that God taught the fundamental truths of religion to the first human beings (*primitive revelation*). This testimony of Scripture has the confirmation of human history, for the belief in one God held by the first men, as Scripture testifies, was the belief of all ancient peoples. It is the clear testimony of historical research that polytheism (belief in several or many gods) was a lapse that came after monotheism (belief in one God). Thus the ancient Babylonians, Assyrians, Egyptians, Chinese, Hindus, Persians, all held to the belief in one God in the earliest times—as their philosophico-religious literature and sacred inscriptions testify—

and only later fell into polytheistic beliefs. The primitive revelation was preserved intact among one people, the Hebrews, from whom the Redeemer was to come. Other peoples quickly lost the revealed truth, transmitted it imperfectly, allowed it to become intermingled with tribal lore and superstitious fables. Among the Hebrews it was conserved by successive new revelations through men divinely sent (prophets, priests, kings, judges). Thus, the true religion was given to man by God in *revelation;* revelation is the origin of religion.

Bringing together the two results of our study, we say that the origin of religion is twofold, viz., the primitive revelation, and man's reason.

Human reason alone would suffice to explain the existence of religion in the world. That a primitive revelation was actually made, does not change that fact. Reason would not suffice, as we shall see, for *all* the requirements of men in the matter of religion; but the fact remains that reason alone would have brought religion—granted an imperfect religion—into being.

Reason itself is a natural revelation. For "revelation" is "the removal or withdrawal of a veil"—of a veil that hangs between man's senses and the invisible causality in things. Reason pierces this veil. Reason recognizes the fact that this changing, limited, contingent, composite world is not self-explanatory; that, in a word, the world is an *effect,* which must have a satisfactory and adequate *cause.* The quest of causes carries reason ultimately to the recognition of a First Cause, itself Uncaused, Infinite, Necessary, All-Perfect. Thus does reason arrive inevitably and infallibly at the fact of God's existence, the basic fact of *religion.* Directly deducible from the existence of the one infinite God, is man's dependence upon Him, and man's duty of knowledge, love, and service toward God. Here, then, is the rational origin of religion.

Thus, speaking absolutely—that is, without taking into account the differences of individual men, their tastes, capacities, and circumstances—the chief fundamental truths of religion must be recognized by reason. Because of this fact St. Paul declared that the pagans were inexcusable for their want of piety. He said that they should have known God and should have given Him honor, because His existence and perfections may be known *by reason* from the facts and phenomena of creation. And again, the Saint said that *the moral law,* as coming from *God,* must be known to all because conscience (i. e., *reason*) bears testimony to its reality. Now the existence of God and the moral law as coming from God are fundamental truths of religion.

In a word, man is inevitably a *religious* being. That man have *reason* is of his essence; and if he use reason, he must recognize religious truths, or, simply, he must recognize *religion.*

b) FALSE THEORIES ABOUT THE ORIGIN OF RELIGION

1. *The Fear Theory.* Primitive men were amazed and frightened by many things. The flash of lightning, the roar of the rolling thunder, the power of the surging sea, the destructive sweep of the forest fire, mysterious disease, the cold and paralyzing unresponsiveness of a dear one dead—all these things stirred man's heart to *fear*. Here were things of terrible character, and their causes and reasons were hidden, invisible. Man came to think of *the invisible causes* of terrifying things as powers that were intelligent, powers that could look upon him and harm him, powers, therefore, that he ought to placate. So man spoke with reverence to these invisible powers of nature, and lo, the first *prayer* was uttered, the first *gods* were recognized, *religion* was born!—Fear cannot account for the origin of religion. Fear is only shrinking from a recognized danger. Fear may indeed quicken the mental faculties and make man *use his reason* feverishly. If fear made primitive men *reason* about the causes of natural phenomena, then *reason,* and not fear, was the origin of religion. Natural phenomena (like lightning, thunder, storms, fires, disease, death) are manifestations of creatures, and they show, as all creatures do, the existence of the Creator. It is altogether possible that the tendency to pray should come strongly upon us when we are afraid; but that is because our *reason* teaches us that God exists, and our fear makes us run to God, just as

a frightened child runs to its parents. But *fear alone*
can teach nothing whatever. Fear is in no wise an in-
structive force. Its reaction upon *reason* may, as we
have said, stir reason to effort, and to intense effort;
but the result is a *reasoned* result, and not a blind
and meaningless conception of new thoughts and
theories. Indeed, fear, inasmuch as it may stir man to
religion, presupposes religious conviction existing in
man's mind *before* fear stirred him to its active recognition. For the rest: if there were anything in the
fear theory of the origin of religion, then non-
reasoning animals would have religion, for such animals can suffer fear even to the extent of panic.

2. *The Fraud Theory.* In early times shrewd men
set themselves up as a priesthood to secure for themselves a place of respect and honor and easy living.
They played upon the credulity of the people, and by
their pseudo-ceremonial of witchcraft or incanta-
tions, aided here and there by fortunate guesses which
passed for true prophecy, they aroused in the minds
of the people a conviction that they were in communi-
cation with an unseen power which ruled the world.
Thus religion came into existence.—A priesthood
presupposes a religion. Nor could a group of leaders,
be they ever so clever, gain such sway over men as
to imprint ineradicably upon the minds of *all peoples
of all times* a false notion of an unseen power. Quack-
ery is ever found within narrow limits of place and
time; truth lives, but error dies. Besides, this theory

takes for granted that primitive men were of absurdly
low mentality, a supposition which, as Ethnology
teaches, is contrary to historical fact. That this theory
is the invention of unbelievers who wish to establish
their case at any cost, even at the cost of self-
contradiction, is obvious from the fact that it declares that there were priests before there was any
religion! This is like saying that there was no Baptism till baptized persons invented it, or that there
was no authority recognized in the world until persons in authority insisted upon its recognition. For
the rest, we have seen that religion is a rational
necessity of man; it is rooted in reason.

3. *The Law Theory.* Legislators in early times
found it necessary, in order to secure reverence for
laws, to appeal to powers of more than earthly authority as their inspiration and support, and to get
current the belief that even undetected offenders
would not escape punishment because their activities
were under the constant inspection of certain all-
seeing eyes. Thus men came to believe in gods. Naturally, too, legislators were held in fear and honor
as the spokesmen of divinities, and they encouraged
more and more the fraudulent religion which elevated their office.—This objection, like the last, is
self-contradictory. How could legislators appeal to
the gods with any hope of success if men did not already believe in gods? This theory presupposes the
existence of the very thing which it pretends to ac-

count for. This objection—again like the last—is
seldom urged nowadays, but it was once in favor
among "unreligionists," and it deserves the notice
we have given it here.

4. *The Ghost Theory.* Sleep was a great mystery
to primitive man. It seemed that it was a state during which an inner man or ghost left the outer visible man unconscious while it journeyed in strange
places. Dreams were but the ill-remembered adven-
tures of the ghost, brought back by the ghost when it
returned to the outer man and caused him to wake.
Then death was but the permanent absence of the
ghost which had often been temporarily absent before, that is, when man slept. In time the conviction
grew general that the ghosts of dead men, particularly
of dead ancestors, continued to have an interest in
earthly things and to exert an unseen power. It were
wise, therefore, to keep these ghosts friendly. Practices of placating ghosts took form; ancestor-worship
appeared among men; *totemism* or belief in the kin-
ship of family, tribe, or clan with a certain genus of
animals or plants appeared. Thus came the cult of
the unseen, and religion.—Historical fact upsets this
fantastic bit of imagination. Many of the lowest and
"most primitive" races had no ancestor-worship, no
trace of totemism, no trace of a ghost-theory at
all, for instance the Pygmies of the Congo. *Totemism, animism* (ancestor-worship) and *fetishism* (be-

lief in a god resident in some bodily object) all explain with many words that man *believed* in such and
such supramundane powers. They do not tell us how
he *began* to believe, unless, indeed, they posit *reason*
as the root of belief, of religion. And then their theory
vanishes, for it is their point to deny the rational
origin of religion. The ghost-theory, in whatever
form it may be understood, makes primitive man less
than a moron in intelligence, it tries to explain the
universal fact of religion by instancing fictitious tribal
beliefs of varying kinds, it contradicts Ethnology,
and it stultifies itself by its assertion that belief in the
unseen began through belief in the unseen.

5. *The Social Theory.* Primitive men, living in
groups, came under the dominance of group-con-
science. They developed a sense of unity in their
group or tribe that made them "herd animals," and
they grew more and more slow to venture upon any
procedure not sanctioned by the group. To such men
group-existence was a thing different from, and
superior to, individual existence. It was but natural
that they should "project" their group-unity or group-
spirit and view it mentally as a kind of high power.
From this it was only a step to the *deification* of
group-unity, group-spirit, group-power. As society
developed, however, the strong sense of group-unity
slackened; men emerged into a clearer consciousness
and appreciation of their individuality. Still, the old

idea of a superior power, a god or gods, endured. The scope of this religious notion was much narrowed and adapted to man's new consciousness of his individual self, and there arose the concept of individual gods.— Among primitives there were many outstanding men, leaders, distinctly individual. Our own American Indians give us a type of primitive civilization, and their brief recorded history is full of the names of great chiefs who were not only warriors, but orators, counsellors of ripe wisdom, some of them inventors of forms of writing for their tribal dialects. The social theory contradicts historical fact, richly increased in our own times by ethnological research, which gives us clear evidence that primitive peoples were not dull masses of witless herd animals. The basic fallacy of this theory is that it makes the individual man among primitives a nonentity, a unit that counts for nothing. There is no shadow of evidence for the assertion of this fallacious notion; its reason for existence lies in the fact that it suits the theory!

6. *The Instinct Theory* (called also the *Prejudice Theory*). Emil Durkheim, leader of a French school of sociology, is largely responsible for this theory. It amounts to this: human societies, like animal societies, obey instincts. *Conscience* and *reason* are only instincts expressed in abstract language. These instinctive common ways of acting have taken such deep root in men that they endure *as ineradicable*

prejudices. Thus consciousness—even reasoned consciousness—of the existence of God and the need of religion is but an inherited prejudice that has nothing to do with fact.—What of the "reason" that worked out this absurd theory? Is that but an instinct "expressed in abstract language"? To what primitive source may we trace the roots of this ineradicable prejudice? And where does the prejudice itself exist outside the narrow limits of the school of Durkheim and his slavish American clientèle? The theory seems to destroy the reason for its own existence. This fallacious theory refuses to see humanity as it is, viz., as an association of individual beings, almost wildly different in character, tastes, temperaments, and views it as a homogeneous mass in which individuality is unknown.

SUMMARY OF THE ARTICLE

In this Article we have briefly indicated the true origin of religion. Then we have outlined and criticized six of the better known theories that are proposed, with small ingenuity, to account for the origin of religion among men. We have found these fallacious theories insufficient. We come back inevitably to the certainty that, if there be any value at all in any human knowledge, the knowledge of God's existence is valid as founded directly upon reason, which works from the facts and phenomena of creation to the one, all-perfect, necessary, infinite Creator. And directly deducible by reason from the existence of the all-perfect God are the truths of man's dependence upon Him, and the necessity of religion.

CHAPTER II

SUPERNATURAL REVELATION IN RELIGION

In the works of creation God reveals Himself and His perfections to man's reason. Since this revelation can be received and recognized by man's unaided natural knowing-powers, it is called *natural* revelation. This Chapter discusses *supernatural* revelation, and asks whether God has manifested truths which lie beyond the scope and grasp of unaided human reason. The assertion that God has done so is made, and is supported by rational argument.

This Chapter explains the meaning of revelation, and discusses the possibility, necessity, and fact of supernatural revelation. These matters are studied in two Articles, as follows:

Article 1. The Meaning, Possibility, and Necessity of Supernatural Revelation

Article 2. The Fact of Supernatural Revelation

Article 1. The Meaning, Possibility, and Necessity of Supernatural Revelation

a) Meaning   b) Possibility   c) Necessity

a) MEANING OF REVELATION

1. *Nominal definition.*—The term *revelation* is derived from the Latin *re-*, "back, from," and *velare*, "to veil," and hence means *the drawing back or re-*

moval of a veil. The word is, therefore, quite suitably employed to indicate the removal of the "veil" of ignorance which hangs between man's knowing-powers and the things which he does not know.

2. *Real definition.*—Revelation is the manifestation of truth hitherto unknown, or known but obscurely. It involves three elements: *a) a revealer,* i. e., one who makes truth known; *b) a truth revealed;* and *c) a recipient* of revelation, i. e., one to whom the revealed truth is manifested. If the *revealer* is man, the revelation is *human;* if the *revealer* is God, the revelation is *divine.*

Divine revelation may be made through the *works* of God, through creation, in such wise as to be available to man's unaided knowing-powers, and then it is *natural* revelation. Again, divine revelation may be made through the *word* of God, and then it is *supernatural* revelation.

It is of supernatural revelation that we speak in the present Article, even when we use the simple term "revelation" without qualifier.

Supernatural revelation may be fully defined as *a manifestation of truth made by Almighty God to rational creatures in a manner other than that which is usual and natural to them in the acquiring of knowledge.*

The *truth* which is revealed is also a determinant in the character of the revelation. If the truth be such that man *could* know it (and perhaps *does* know it) without supernatural revelation, but is nevertheless supernaturally revealed, it makes the revelation *supernatural in manner,* but not in *substance.* If, however, the truth revealed be of such character that man could not possibly know it without revelation, then the revelation is *supernatural in substance* as well as *in manner.* To illustrate: that God exists, man knows by reason arguing from the data of creation; this naturally known truth is also supernaturally revealed; such revelation is *supernatural in manner only* (i. e., in the manner of its manifestation). That God is one infinite and undivided substance subsisting in Three Persons, is a truth which man could not know unless it were divinely revealed; therefore, its revelation is *supernatural in substance as well as in manner.* Sometimes the term *in form* is used for *in manner.*

b) POSSIBILITY OF SUPERNATURAL REVELATION

If a thing is *not* possible, this is inevitably due to one of two reasons, viz., (*a*) there is a contradiction in the very concept or idea of the thing itself, or (*b*) there is in existence no power great enough to produce, or make, or do the thing. A "square circle" is impossible by the first of these reasons; it is a contradiction in itself; one part of it is a denial of the other, and the result is zero. There is nothing impossible by the second reason if we include the boundless power of Almighty God in our concept of *existing powers* capable of producing effects. But if there is any *indignity, unworthiness, uselessness* about the thing, then the boundless power of God cannot produce it, for God is all-perfect, and an unworthy thing would not square with His majesty and dignity; while a useless thing would not square with God's wisdom. Hence, *absolutely* speaking God's power is boundless and can produce anything that is a *thing* and not a *contradiction,* which is *nothing;* but *relatively* speaking (i. e., with *relation* to God's all-perfect nature) certain things which are possible in view of God's power are not possible in view of His other perfections. We usually put this in another way, and say that all things are possible to God's *absolute power,* but not all things are possible to God's *relative power.*

Now we investigate the subject of supernatural revelation, asking whether it be possible. Certainly, it is possible to God's absolute power; it is the revealing of truth, and God knows all truth and has the power to manifest it. But is it possible to God's relative power? Is there not some indignity in the thought of the all-perfect God revealing truths to men? Not at all; it is no indignity for the wisest teacher to instruct the most ignorant and backward pupil; such an action rather adds to the opinion we hold of the wise teacher: we respect his great knowledge, and when we find him instructing the ignorant we love him for his great kindness. Therefore, there is no

indignity in the thought of God teaching men, no unworthiness in such a thought.—But is not revelation
a mark of unwisdom in God? Is it not an evidence that
His work of creation is imperfect and incomplete,
and that He seeks to correct first omissions by subsequent instructions divinely revealed? God has His
own ends; He is not bound to make a thing absolutely
perfect in its order, but His wisdom requires that it
have that perfection which will make it suited, and
admirably suited, to attain the end it was made for.
God is not bound to "exhaust" His powers at creation; it belongs to His perfection that He be free to
make something new, teach something new, at any
time He chooses. Hence revelation is not contrary to
God's wisdom.—But is not revelation useless? How
can finite man receive instruction from the infinite?
Is it not useless then for the infinite to attempt to
reveal truth to finite minds? This objection is rather
silly at best. Could not a finite thing stand in the light
that poured from an infinite source (if such a source
were possible for material light)? Man's nature is
capable of receiving instruction, man needs instruction; he can receive, according to his capacity, the
instruction of even an infinite teacher. The mind of
man can grasp truth; it cannot, indeed, have *exhaus-
tive* knowledge of boundless truth, but it can have
knowledge that is quite clear, definite, and distinct, as
far as it goes. To illustrate by a rough analogy : a pic-

ture of a man's face may be beautifully clear and distinct, and it is not an argument against its clarity to say that the picture is not an image of the entire man.

We may sum up the whole matter in this way : Revelation is possible if there is nothing to thwart it : (a) on the part of God, the Revealer, or (b) on the part of man, the recipient of the revelation, or (c) on the part of the truth revealed. Now there is nothing to thwart revelation on the part of God, for it does not contradict His wisdom nor His majesty, and He knows all truth and can manifest it as He will. Nor is there anything to thwart revelation on the part of man, for man's nature is capable of receiving instruction ; man craves knowledge of the truth and can receive it in the measure of his own capacity, even if it come from an infinite source. Finally, there is nothing to thwart revelation on the part of the truth revealed, for truth is essentially a thing that may be manifested. We conclude, then, that revelation is possible.

Nay, revelation is not only possible, but *probable*. We shall presently seek proofs of revelation as a fact, but, even before considering such proofs, we may assert here that the goodness and love of the all-perfect Creator toward His children would naturally take form in communications to help and guide them on their journey toward their last end.

c) THE NECESSITY OF SUPERNATURAL REVELATION

In the order of existence, a being is *necessary* when it is so perfect that it must exist and cannot not-exist. Thus, God is necessary being—the *only* necessary being. But in the order of *requisites* for being or action, that is *necessary* which is indispensable, and without which the being or action cannot exist, or, at least, cannot exist perfectly. It is in the latter sense that we use the term *necessary* (and *necessity*) in the present study.

We speak here of supernatural revelation as requisite for man's knowledge of the truths, laws, and practices which constitute objective religion. We have already seen that man has the indispensable obligation of practising religion in order to fulfill the purpose of his being and reach the end for which he was created. Now we say that without revelation man cannot fully know nor well perform his duty of religion. In a word, we say that revelation is *necessary*.

There are degrees of necessity. A thing may be so indispensable that there is simply no doing without it, and then it is said to be *absolutely* necessary. Again, a thing may be requisite in the sense that to do without it would be extremely difficult, and even well nigh impossible, and then it is said to be *morally* necessary.

We assert: (1) That supernatural revelation is *absolutely* necessary for the knowledge of the truths of supernatural religion strictly so called; (2) That supernatural revelation is *morally* necessary for the adequate knowledge of the truths of natural religion. We offer evidence for each assertion:

1. *Revelation is absolutely necessary* for the knowledge of the truths of supernatural religion, strictly so called (i. e., truths that are supernatural *in substance* as well as *in manner*). This assertion is so obvious that it scarcely needs proof. For such truths as we here discuss are precisely those truths that man's reason cannot work out from the data of creation. If such truths be not revealed, there is no conceivable way in which man can know them. Revelation is, therefore, *absolutely* necessary for the knowledge of such truths.

2. *Revelation is morally necessary* for the adequate knowledge of the truths of natural religion. For, although man's reason *could,* theoretically speaking, work out these truths from the data of creation, still, in practice, it is certain that reason *would not* do so. There is great difficulty in the work; and the result would surely be imperfect in any case. We allege *difficulty* and *imperfection,* therefore, as our reasons for declaring man's reason practically insufficient for the attainment of the entire and perfect knowledge of natural religion; and for the same reason we declare revelation morally necessary. Let us look at the matter more closely:

a) It would be *difficult* for man to work out the truths of natural religion by reasoning from the data of creation. All men, indeed, may easily know the existence of God, but the religious truths that are reasoned from God's existence are arrived at by a process of thought that is at once abstruse and complicated. Not all men have the ability and the education requisite for following and understanding such a process of thought, much less for inaugurating it. And even if man had the ability, it would take long years of study for him to discover all the truths of natural religion; and during those very years he is under strict obligation to practise religion! But even if man had the ability to know all the truths of natural religion in a very brief time, many men would not do so. For many have no taste for serious constructive thought; many others have literally no time for it, so closely are they occupied with the tasks of daily life, the work of obtaining means for food, shelter, and clothing for themselves and their families. Thus, taking the human race by and large, it is quite evident that difficulties which are well nigh insurmountable prevent men from obtaining by natural powers the full knowledge of natural religion. Thus are we justified in declaring that for such full knowledge *revelation is morally necessary.*

b) If man were to work out all the truths of natural religion, surmounting unaided every difficulty, his work would still be *imperfect* and, in so far, unsuitable for helping him to achieve his last end, which is the very function of religion. For man is likely to make mistakes in his most careful study; error would almost unquestionably be admixed with the truths discovered. As a matter of fact, not one of the greatest of human thinkers, not Plato, not Aristotle, ever achieved a perfect exposition of natural religion. What, then, would be the achievement of the average man? And should a man really attain to a perfect knowledge of natural religion by his unaided efforts, his work would still be imperfect in point of authority. He could not pass it on to others as a completed work. For others might well say, "Why should we accept this man's word? He is fallible like ourselves." And even if the work were perfectly reasoned out and perfectly expressed, it would yet require the individual study (a long hard term of it) and approval of each and every man that accepted it. Divine revelation, with its unquestionable authority, is morally necessary for the full and complete knowledge of the truths of the natural religion.

SUMMARY OF THE ARTICLE

In this Article we have studied the meaning of *revelation*, defining it both as a *name* and as a *reality*. We have distinguished revelation as *human* and *divine;* and divine revelation we have distinguished as *natural* and *supernatural*. We have discussed the possibility of revelation, and have seen that there is nothing to render it impossible on the part of *God, the revealer,* or of *man, the recipient* of revealed truth, or of *the truth itself* that is revealed. We have asserted the necessity of revelation, and, after a preliminary discussion of *necessity,* have seen clear and convincing evidence that supernatural revelation is *absolutely necessary* for a knowledge of the truths of supernatural religion, while it is *morally necessary* for a knowledge of the truths of the natural religion.

ARTICLE 2. THE FACT OF SUPERNATURAL REVELATION

a) The Criteria of Revelation   b) Holy Scripture
c) Tradition

a) THE CRITERIA OF REVELATION

Revelation, which is morally necessary to man, must, if it be given, show unmistakable *signs or marks* which evidence it as true supernatural revelation. Such signs or marks are known as the *criteria* of revelation. The word *criteria* is the plural of *criterion,* a Greek word that has been taken bodily into the English language; it signifies "a means for judging." The *criteria* of revelation are, therefore, the means for judging revelation and knowing for certain that it is truly revelation and not a pretended, fictitious, or counterfeit manifestation of doctrine.

The criteria of revelation are both *internal* and *external.* Internal criteria are those that are contained in the doctrine itself which claims to be revealed. External criteria are remarkable signs, outside the doctrine revealed, which point to it and mark it as the actual revelation of God. We shall speak of both kinds of criteria in some detail:

1. *Internal Criteria of Revelation.*—One of the fonts of revelation, as we shall presently see, is Holy Scripture or the Bible. The Bible is offered to men as the word of God; it is a body of matters *revealed*. Now, in looking for the *internal criteria* of the Bible we ask: What is the nature of the contents of this scripture? Is it noble, majestic, calculated to raise and satisfy man's best aspirations, beneficial to man and to society? Does it bear the mark of superhuman wisdom? Nay, is it such that man, unaided by God, could not have produced it? If so, then there is internal evidence of compelling nature to induce us to accept it as the very word of God. In a word, the *internal criteria* declare it to be a body of true supernatural revelation.—Internal criteria are recognized as of the greatest value in determining the age, authorship, and genuineness of many merely human documents and monuments. Study of the internal structure, style, and content of a manuscript may often give us certain knowledge of its age and authorship. For example, archæologists have made certain (largely by internal criteria) that the "Moabite Stone" was engraved in the 9th century B. C. Paintings left unsigned by ancient masters have often been

identified beyond question by their internal criteria
(e. g., style, manner of workmanship, quality of
coloring, method in which the oils have been applied,
treatment of line and perspective, etc.). On the other
hand, many manuscripts and paintings which present
spurious claims of noted authorship are shown to be
counterfeit by the study of internal criteria. No one
can deny that the study of such criteria is a scientific
procedure and one of immense value. True, the matter
is open to abuse, and man's tendency to be precipitate
in pronouncing judgment may, in certain cases, rob it
of significance. Thus a poem written by James Whitcomb Riley was once foisted successfully on the best
critics as a newly discovered relic of Edgar Allan
Poe. This was possible because the poem was written by a real poet, comparable with the other whose
work he had imitated. But had the "discovery" been
the composition of a young schoolboy, there would
have been no doubt or deception to affect the critics.
Now, if a sacred writing be as distinct and different
in content from the works of men as the best poetry
of Poe is distinct and different from the random
rhymes of a schoolboy, then it is certain beyond doubt
or scruple that men are not its sole and sufficient
authors. That such compelling criteria exist to sub-
stantiate the claims of Holy Scripture to be true revelation, it will be our task presently to prove. Here
we simply indicate the nature of internal criteria and
declare its value as a determinant of authorship.

2. *External Criteria of Revelation.*—The external criteria of revelation are (*a*) Miracles and (*b*) Prophecies. If true miracles are wrought, if true prophecies are pronounced and perfectly fulfilled, in support of the claims of a revelation, then it is certain that such revelation is indeed God's very word; for miracles and prophecies are works of God and of no other. They are the "seals" which God alone can impress upon a doctrine, and they indicate "the genuine article." We shall speak briefly about each of these criteria:

a) *Miracles* are marvellous events, outside the ordinary course of nature, produced by Almighty God. Now, there are two questions that may be raised about miracles: Are miracles possible? If possible, do they really occur, or have they occurred? To the first question we must give an affirmative answer, or show upon what score miracles are impossible. Surely they are not impossible to God, for God can do anything in which there is no contradiction, and in miracles there is no such contradiction. Neither do miracles contradict the divine wisdom; they are not "corrections" or "unforeseen prodigies" wrought by God in unexpected circumstances: they are exceptions to the uniform way in which things act (i. e., to "natural laws"), but God who framed the mode of action of creatures can also decree exceptions *from eternity;* and thus the miracle is as much a part of the eternal and changeless decrees of God as the regular course

of nature. Nor is there any impossibility in miracles
inasmuch as they affect creatures; for creatures are
utterly dependent and contingent, and can make no
"demands" to be left in the ordinary course of their
natural action. In the abstract, then, miracles are certainly possible. But do they occur? Certain smug
gentlemen of the last century thought they were saying something very wise and scientific when they
placidly announced that "Miracles simply do not happen." The answer to that blind assertion is simply that
miracles *have* occurred, and, as a matter of fact, *do*
occur. When, for example, a gaping wound is *suddenly* healed, we have a miracle. When a dead man is
raised to life, we have a miracle. Take the case of the
wound suddenly healed. Nature as we know it would
have to be entirely reconstructed to produce such as
effect without miracle; therefore, there can be no
question of a "hidden law of nature of which we are
yet ignorant" as an explanation of such a result. Nature heals wounds, but it requires in every case the
coöperation of time, and a good deal of time too. Cell
comes from cell; protoplasm from protoplasm. The
process is very gradual. In the case considered there is
no such gradual process, but an immediate and perfect healing. Here, then, is an unquestioned "marvellous event outside the ordinary course of nature."
That God is its author may be known from the human
agent through whom the wonder is wrought, his purpose, his character, the effect he desires to produce by

the act. If there be certainty of the good moral effect of the events, and of the good aim and character of the person through whom the wondrous deed is wrought, we have no choice but to declare that the miracle is a true one and that God is its author. Certain deceptive effects may be produced by trickery; obviously, there is no question of such matters here, for investigation and scientific procedure can always discover the true source of such effects. Again, preternatural powers that are evil—devils, in a word—may produce wondrous effects, but, as the fruit shows the tree, so such effects show their evil source. Besides, evil spirits are not omnipotent; there are some effects that are entirely outside their power to produce. We come back to the fact that miracles can and do happen, and that they can be known as true miracles. At Lourdes—to name but one place where miracles have occurred and occur still—there is a corps of physicians and surgeons in attendance, among them men of no faith who would like nothing better than to explain the miracles by natural causes, and yet all are forced to admit that the miracles happen. Most of the miracles there recorded are immediate cures of organic ailments, restoration of tissues that could be restored in no natural way without the protracted co-operation of time and careful treatment. Less than fourteen percent of the miracles there scientifically recorded are of such kind that they *could* have a possible explanation in nervous shock and sudden readjustment of muscular and nervous function. If there is any human certainty about events, if there is any certainty about causes and effects, if there is any certainty at all, the sincere mind is literally forced to admit not only the *possibility*, but the actual *fact*, of the existence of true miracles. And miracles, by their very definition are works of God. Now, when God works a miracle as a seal and signature of some doctrine, then that doctrine must be, beyond quibble, the very word of God Himself.

b) *Prophecies* are certain and definite predictions of events which depend for their occurrence upon free-will (whether of God or men), and so cannot be merely guessed at or conjectured with anything approaching certainty. Prophecies are sure predictions of future free events. In other words, they are predictions of future events which only Omniscience can know. Therefore, they are proper to God, and when God signs a doctrine with prophecies that are perfectly fulfilled, the doctrine is the word of God.

b) HOLY SCRIPTURE

Holy Scripture, or the Bible, is one of the fonts of revelation. *Bible* (from the Greek *ta biblia,* "the books") is the name of a collection of writings which the Church recognizes as the true word of God. It is divided into the *Old Testament,* or books written before the coming of Our Lord, and the *New Testament* or sacred writings composed after the coming

of Christ. That the Bible is true revelation we know
by internal and external criteria. We cannot here go
into details about the various parts of the Old and
New Testaments, but present our arguments *in general*. However, we give a somewhat detailed description of the Old and New Testament writings and
their authenticity in the Appendix of this book.

1. *Internal Criteria.* The Bible, in both Old and
New Testaments, possesses a *unity* and *beauty* absolutely unique among known writings. Made up of
widely various matters, written by writers of every
degree of culture and education, composed in many
different times and places, set forth in varied forms
of classic language and dialect, it nevertheless possesses an organic unity that binds together all the
integral parts of the volume and sets forth in most
regular process the unfolding of a plan that centers
in the person and the work of Our Divine Lord. In
no merely human book are such unity and beauty discerned. One writer, equipped for his work by careful training and long study, may succeed in producing
a very harmonious and unified work; and yet his
work (if we look for it among existing books) does
not present such unity and beauty as this *collection*
of widely various compositions, made by different
men, of different abilities, in different times, in different places, and through the medium of different
forms of speech. Even here we have evidence of a
more than human authorship in the Holy Scriptures.

Surely one Mind conceived and executed this unified
work.—But leaving aside unity and beauty of style
and structure, let us consider the *influence* exercised
by this sacred volume. It is not its literary value and
power that have made the Bible the one almost universal influence over minds and hearts that it has
been through the centuries; no, it is the very *content*
of the Scripture. As a consolation in trial, as a monu-
ment of the teaching received from the Apostles, as a
source of hope and courage in face of temptation, as
an oracle of God to turn to upon every occasion, the
Holy Scripture stands absolutely *unique* among the
books available to men.—Again,—to choose but one
instance of compelling internal evidence,—if we but
study the utterances of Christ as recorded in the New
Testament, we must be convinced that these are the
very words of God; for no solemn pronouncement of
scholar, or hero, or philosopher, can compare in
dignity, majesty, power, superhuman understanding
of life and human hearts, with the words of One
who (considered as man) had no worldly education,
no training in mighty thoughts and ideals for the
guidance of the destinies of men and of the world.
If we read the bald narrative of Scripture, and dwell
upon the words of Our Lord, we must needs para-
phrase the exclamation of the soldier at the Crucifixion and cry out from the depths of a sincerely convinced mind, "Indeed this is the Word of God!"
In Holy Scripture, then, Revelation is a fact.

2. *External Criteria.* The *prophecies* contained in
both Old and New Testaments are numerous, and are
fulfilled in fact. The most important of the Old Testament prophecies are those that foretell the coming of
the Redeemer; and these deal in no generalities, but
are clear and full of detail and circumstance. Thus the
date of the Redeemer's coming was foretold (Daniel ix, 24), as was the fact that He was to be *born
of a virgin* (Isaias vii, 14), of the tribe of *family of
David* (Jeremias xxiii, 5), *at Bethlehem* (Micheas
v, 2), and that kings should come offering Him gifts
(Psalm lxii, 9). To mention other prophecies: the
name of the Redeemer was foretold; His Passion and
death were described; the fact that He was to be
sold for thirty pieces of silver, that He was to have
hands and feet pierced, that His garments were to
be distributed, and His outer garment assigned by
lot, that he was to rise again, to pour out His spirit
on all men, and establish a kingdom that should not
be destroyed—all these facts and many others were
foretold in the Old Testament from 400 to 800 years
before they occurred. In the New Testament, too, we
find prophecies, chief of which were pronounced by
Our Lord Himself. He foretold the manner and time
of His Death, His Resurrection, His Ascension. He
foretold that Judas would betray Him, that Peter
would deny Him, that His disciples would forsake
Him, that the Holy Ghost would come upon the
disciples. He foretold the destruction of Jerusalem,

the razing of the Temple, the dispersion of the Jews. He foretold the growth of His Church and the preaching of His gospel to all men.—Thus, true prophecies attest the character of Holy Scripture as genuine revelation. *In Holy Scripture, then, revelation is a fact.*

c) TRADITION

Tradition, as we employ the word, does not mean a haphazard handing on of doctrine from father to son, from generation to generation. It means the word of God that was not committed to inspired writings, but nevertheless was set forth in uninspired writings of genuine historical value and in other monuments the reliability of which cannot be questioned. It is supplementary to Holy Scripture, and *together with Scripture* constitutes the sole source of general divine revelation.

The Apostles preached under God's guidance, and their words were confirmed by "signs that followed," i. e., by miracles. In like manner, God's guidance is discerned in the doctrinal and liturgical practices of the Church, for the Church was founded by God-made-Man, and He promised to abide with it forever, to keep it from leading men astray and to make it lead souls to God, their last end. Thus, we find reliable *Tradition* in (*a*) the Apostolic preaching and instruction; (*b*) the doctrinal and liturgical practice of the Church; (*c*) the writings of holy and learned men who lived and wrote in the early centuries of Christianity (i. e., the Fathers of the Church) ; for such writings reflect Apostolic teaching, since the writers were pious men, in close contact with one another and with the bishops of the Church, and could not have introduced new and unauthoritative doctrines in their writings (even on the impossible supposition that they would try to do so) without immediate detection and condemnation; (d) the *liturgy,* and *acts of the martyrs,* and the *creeds* or formulas of faith recognized and used by the Church.

Our Lord Jesus Christ is true God (as we shall prove in the next Book of Apologetics) and His revelation is true revelation; it is the true word of God. Now Our Lord made provision for the propagation and preservation of His revealed religion by commissioning His Apostles to speak and teach in His name. He told them to teach "all things whatsoever He had commanded them." Hence, the Apostolic teaching is true revelation; it is the instruction of Christ Himself, imparted to the world through the Apostles; and Christ told His Apostles that "he that heareth you, heareth me, and he that heareth me, heareth him that sent me." Now this revelation, this teaching or word of God Himself, was made known to the world not only in the Holy Scriptures, but in *Tradition.* St. Clement of Rome, writing before the year 100, declared that the Apostles arranged for the continuance of their work after their own deaths by

a succession of authorized teachers. St. Irenaeus
wrote, in the second century, that every sincere in-
quirer after truth might know it from "the tradition
of the Apostles, which is known to all the world."
St. Paul commanded the Thessalonians (2 Thess. ii,
14) to "hold the traditions which you have learned
whether by word or by our epistle." Certainly, the
Apostles did not all write; only two of the Apostles
wrote Gospels (SS. Matthew and John), but all
taught, and the teaching of all was equally the word
of God. Besides, the Scripture, despite its perfection,
is not a sufficient revelation of *all* truths of the supernatural religion. Without Tradition we should not
know what Scripture is, what books belong to it, nor
the proper interpretation of its contents. Those that
say that the Bible alone is the source of all revealed
truth will search the Bible in vain for the support of
their assertion.

Two things are, therefore, certain: first, the teaching of the Apostles was the true word of God, was
revelation; and secondly, this teaching is embodied
in Tradition. If, then, it can be shown that Tradition
has been kept intact, it follows of necessity that
revelation as a fact is contained in Tradition.

Now Tradition was and is kept intact. The successors of the Apostles, the bishops, were, from the
earliest days of the Church, in close contact with one
another and with the Pope, the successor of St. Peter.
If any individual held an erroneous view, this was

known and condemned at once. The vital importance
of holding the true faith made the subject of the
"content" of the faith of deepest interest and concern to all Christians; and nothing new or unauthor-
ized could creep in without instant detection.

In passing, we mention that the dogmas pronounced by the Church through all ages are never
new truths. Dogmas are pronounced to settle the question that sometimes arises about a doctrine held by all,
but about the *origin* of which there is dispute. In other
words, a doctrine ever believed by the Church may
sometimes come into question as to whether it is
really revealed or whether, perhaps, it has been held as
a pious belief, a logical doctrine in view of the body
of truths delivered to the Apostles (i. e., "the De-
posit of Faith"). Thus new pronouncements of doctrine, new dogmas, are authoritative settlements of
points concerning the *standing* of doctrines: they
are never new or "newly invented" doctrines. Revelation of the necessary truths of the faith was definitely closed with the death of the last Apostle; but
it is in the very nature of things that there should be
occasional question about the content of that revelation, question of this or that point of doctrine as belonging or not belonging to that revelation. From this
passing remark we may see at once that while Holy
Scripture and Tradition constitute the sole source of
revealed doctrine, they need an authoritative inter-

preter; and this, as we shall see by and by, is the infallible Church of Christ and its infallible Head. In a word, Scripture and Tradition are the complete *font of revelation,* but they are not the complete *rule of faith.* The rule of faith is the teaching of the Church divinely founded to show men *infallibly* the way of truth and of salvation.

In this Article we have studied the *criteria* of revelation, both *internal* and *external,* and have seen that such criteria are valuable, and when verified are sufficient to compel assent and cause one to recognize revelation as the true and indubitable word of God. We have studied in short detail the external criteria of revelation, viz., *miracles* and *prophecies* both as *possibilities* and as *facts.* We have briefly studied *Holy Scripture* and *Tradition* and have seen that these are justified by the *criteria* as true revelation.

BOOK THIRD

CHRIST

In Book First we proved that there exists one, infinite, all-perfect God, who is the Creator, Preserver, and Ruler of the universe. In Book Second we showed that this all-perfect God is to be known, loved, and served by men in the practice of the true religion. In this Third Book we study Him who brought the true religion to men, Jesus Christ, man's *Redeemer,* who is both *true God* and *true man.* The Book is divided into three Chapters as follows:

Chapter   I. Jesus Christ, the Redeemer
Chapter II. Jesus Christ, True God
Chapter III. Jesus Christ, True Man

JESUS CHRIST, THE REDEEMER

This Chapter deals with the fact that man, created and preserved by God for the attainment of a wondrous end through the practice of true religion, is not as God made him, but has fallen from pristine perfection and requires a *redemption* to restore to him his lost opportunity of achieving his end. Further, the Chapter studies the fact that this necessary redemption has been accomplished by Jesus Christ, who is, in consequence, the true *Redeemer*.

The Chapter is accordingly divided into two Articles as follows:

Article 1. The Redemption
Article 2. The Redeemer

Article 1. The Redemption

a) Meaning of Redemption   b) The Need of Redemption
c) The Fact of Redemption

a) MEANING OF *REDEMPTION*

The term *redemption* (from the Latin *re-*, "back," and *emere* "to buy") means the *act of buying back*. This nominal definition squares well with the real definition of the term; for the real meaning of the Redemption is *the act by which the God-Man bought back for mankind the opportunity lost by original sin,* viz., the opportunity of attaining God and eternal happiness. The *price* paid for this purchase was the sufferings and death of the Redeemer.

b) THE NEED OF REDEMPTION

There is need of *buying back* only when a necessary thing has been lost or thrown away and cannot be recovered without the payment of a price. Now, by original sin man threw away his necessary opportunity of achieving God and Heaven; nor can man regain that opportunity except through the payment of an adequate price. By reason of original sin, therefore, redemption is necessary. To show the value of this reasoning we must study 1. Original Sin as a Fact; and 2. The Price Required to Restore the Opportunity Lost by Original Sin.

1. *Original Sin as a Fact.*—We turn to Holy Scripture for an account of man's first sin and its effect upon the human race; but reason and daily experience furnish an irrefragable confirmation of the same facts. While there is no purely rational *proof* of original sin apart from revelation, there is everything in human nature and in the experiences of life to suggest it, nay, to insist upon it. So true is this that one of the most clear-headed thinkers of our times has gone so far as to say that original sin is "the only part of Christian theology which can really be proved." His meaning is, of course, that this is, of all truths, the most evident in the inner and outer life of

men, and is thus inevitably proved, even though a rational demonstration may not be formulated in metaphysical terms. For, if one clear demonstration cannot be made by reason alone, there are a million conditions, thoughts, emotions, feelings, situations, and traditions, which make the matter one that is impossible to deny.

Consider the following remarks by Mr. G. K. Chesterton (*The Everlasting Man*, p. 42, and p. 98) : ". . . original sin is really original. Not merely in theology but in history it is a thing rooted in the origins. Whatever else men have believed, they have all believed that *there is something the matter with mankind.* The sense of sin has made it impossible to be natural and have no clothes, just as it has made it impossible to be natural and have no laws." ". . . there is a feeling [in the ancient pagans] that there is something higher than the gods; but because it is higher, it is also further away. Not yet could even Virgil have read the riddle and the paradox of that other divinity who is both higher and nearer. For them what was truly divine was very distant. . . . It had less and less to do with . . . mere mythology. Yet even in this there was a sort of tacit admission of its intangible purity, when we consider what most of the mythology is like. . . . In other words, there is something in the whole tone of the time suggesting that men had accepted a lower level, and were still half-conscious that it was a lower level.

It is hard to find words for these things; yet the one really just word stands ready. *These men were conscious of the Fall,* if they were conscious of nothing else; and the same is true of all heathen humanity."

Consider also the following remarks of the same gifted thinker (*Orthodoxy,* p. 24 f. and p. 268): "Certain new theologians dispute original sin, which is the only part of Christian theology which can really be proved. Some followers of the Rev. R. J. Campbell . . . admit divine sinlessness, which they cannot see even in their dreams. But they essentially deny human sin which they can see in the street. The strongest saints and the strongest sceptics alike took positive evil as the starting-point of their argument. If it be true (as it certainly is) that a man can feel exquisite happiness in skinning a cat, then the religious philosopher can only draw one of two conclusions. He must either deny the existence of God, as all atheists do; or he must deny *the present union between God and man,* as all Christians do. The new theologians seem to think it a highly rationalistic solution to deny the cat."—"Science knows nothing whatever about pre-historic man; for the excellent reason that he is pre-historic. A few professors choose to conjecture that such things as human sacrifice were once innocent and general and that they gradually dwindled; but there is no direct evidence of it, and the small amount of indirect evidence is very much the other way. In the earliest legends we have, such as the tales of Isaac and Iphigenia, human sacrifice is not introduced as something old, but rather as something new; as a strange and frightful exception darkly demanded by the gods. History says nothing; and the legends all say that the earth was kinder in its earliest time. There is no tradition of progress; but *the whole human race has a tradition of the Fall.* Amusingly enough, the very dissemination of this idea is used against its authenticity. Learned men literally say that this pre-historic calamity cannot be true because every race of mankind remembers it. I cannot keep pace with these paradoxes."

The following points, chosen out of a thousand that could be mentioned, are listed as suggestions for thought upon the obvious character of original sin as a fact in human existence : (*a*) the phenomenon of shame with reference to the physical root-realities of our being; (*b*) the traditions of ancient peoples about a rebellion of men against God, as in the story of Prometheus and the Titans; in purifications as requisite for the newly blessed mother of children; in the notion that man had some former spiritual existence and was put into a body-prison in punishment for some primal sin; (*c*) the consciousness of miseries as *punishments*—a favorite idea with poets, philosophers, and people in all ancient times from Homer and Hesiod and Plato downward; (*d*) the various traditions of some Paradise Lost—Elysium, the Isles of the Blessed, Atlantis, the Golden Age, etc.;

(*e*) the consciousness common to all men of a tendency to do wrong even in defiance of the knowledge of what is right. All these things show that "there is something the matter with mankind," that something valuable has been lost through man's own fault, and that he is suffering for it, that man has thrown something away and is hapless without it; in a word, *that original sin is a fact*.

Original sin was the failure of man at some primal trial. Holy Scripture (*Book of Genesis*) gives a detailed account of man's trial and failure. The word of Scripture is the word of God, and Scripture is moreover a reliable historical document, humanly considered. Therefore, we must accept the Scriptural testimony. Still, even if Scripture had nothing to tell us in this matter, reason would assure us that some such trial must have taken place, even as experience and the common consciousness of the race assure us that man failed in the trial. It is interesting and profitable for us to consider what human reason has to say on this subject, and we proceed to do so.

Reason asserts that man's faculties (i. e., capacities for action) and, in particular, man's finest and noblest faculties, were given to him that he might use them in the attainment of his last end, the purpose of his being. Now, man's noblest faculties are his *intellect* or understanding and his *free-will*. By these, above other faculties of minor nature, man was meant to attain to God and Heaven, his last end. But

man exercises the faculty of intellect by acquiring
rational knowledge; and he exercises free-will by
choosing what that knowledge evidences to him as
good. To achieve God, therefore, man had to know
God and God's will, and freely choose to love God
and perform God's will. Therefore, the very first
man, the father of all, had to represent his race, as he,
in a manner, contained his race. He had to have some
perfectly free opportunity of choosing or rejecting
God—otherwise, in spite of the splendid faculties of
intellect and free-will, man would be necessitated in
his acts, and his finest faculties would be vain and
useless. In a word, man had to stand some test, some
trial, where his faculties of intellect and free-will
would be exercised as they should be, or, if man
freely proved perverse, as they should *not be*. Man
failed in the trial. Original sin became a fact. And by
original sin—the first man outraged and defiled his
nature; he rejected the true end of his being; he
forfeited the supernatural gifts and helps with which
the Creator had provided him. As a result, man stood
in the world as an alien and an outcast, an exile ban-
ished from his true home, unable to attain or to claim
the end for which he had been made. Crippled in the
finest faculties of his being, stripped of supernatural
aids, his birthright sold and forfeited, man was
literally in the state of a cripple who stands at the
foot of a stairway which he is unable to climb, looking helplessly upward to a door which he longs to

enter, but which his own perversity has closed and locked against him. His need is twofold: he requires help up the stairway, and he requires that the door at the head of the stairway be opened again to him. For these needs to be supplied, man required *a redeemer,* who would open heaven (the locked door), and give him help to get there (help up the stairway).

Now, man outraged his nature, injuring its finest faculties, by the original sin. And this injured nature he passed on to his descendants. The first man forfeited God and happiness. The forfeit affected all of his descendants. Just as a father whose wealth is immense may leave his children poor (even though it is no fault of their own) by squandering his goods, so did the first parent leave his children poor by squandering the unspeakably great and valuable goods of supernatural grace and natural perfections.

A question may here arise. It will be admitted that man must have had some primal trial. It will be admitted that man failed at the trial. It will be admitted that every race of mankind has an inner consciousness of that failure. But is there not some further word to be said, to show that all men of all races are truly children of the one father who sinned in the beginning? Such a further word shall indeed be said.

The whole of mankind is descended from a single pair of parents, and this is the fact indicated in the expressions, *the solidarity of the human race,* and *the unity of the human race.* Despite various vague evolutionary doctrines, the assertion of this unity is scientific. For consider: human beings are specifically the same; human nature is the same in men of all colors, cultures, dispositions; all men have the same physiological and psychological operations, the same laws of generation and birth, the same facility of inter-racial fecundity, the same power of reasoning, the same faculty of speech, the same moral conscience, the same need of religion. Thus is the revealed doctrine that a *single pair of human parents* is the source of all mankind, corroborated by the findings of science. Further, the common consciousness of *all* men of the original shipwreck of human nature is a strong, a compelling, argument for the fact that all men are of one single stock.

Two things then are certain: (*a*) The first man sinned, and (*b*) The first man is the father of all men. In him all sinned, for in him, in a manner, all men were contained. The injured nature of the first sinful man came to all men. Even as the first man required a redeemer, so do all men require a redeemer.

In passing, we must mention the fact that the Blessed Virgin Mary *was kept immune* from the common heritage of original sin, and was never, at any moment, stained with its guilt. It is unthinkable that the maternal source of the human nature of the God-Man should be *in any way whatever* tainted or evil. We call this exemption of the Blessed Mother her *Immaculate Conception,* and declare it to be an immunity from all trace of original sin, wrought in her behalf by the special providence of God, in view of the merits to be won by her Divine Son. The matter is divinely revealed, but, as we see here, it is also clearly approved by reason.

2. *The Price Required to Restore the Opportunity Lost by Original Sin.*—If man was to have the opportunity of attaining his last end *restored to him,* a price had to be paid for that restoration. God could, indeed, by His absolute power, have forgiven the sin outright; but this would have been in conflict with divine wisdom. For, had no price been exacted, no man could ever *earn* the attainment of his last end. The greatest virtue, the most sublime devotion, the most unflagging service to God, could never *deserve* a reward; man could never *merit,* never *earn* any grace. He might indeed, God freely bestowing the first grace, establish a kind of claim to further grace by good use of the first, but this claim would not be a claim *in strict justice.* Now, we know that divine love and wisdom wishes man, if he is to attain his end at all, to *work out,* to *earn,* his way thereto. A rich and kind employer hires a laborer; the laborer cannot earn the position, but once he is given the place, given the work to do and the tools required to do it, he can *earn* recompense. Surely the kind employer does not wish it otherwise. God made man in His image to live here on earth and work out his salvation, the purpose of his being. Man could not earn existence,

nor could he earn the first grace, but given these, surely he could earn recompense of further grace for the good use he made of the first. Man sinned. God could have left him so, reduced in sin, his end unachievable. But revelation, as well as the voice of human hearts speaking universally, proclaims that God did not leave man so. He promised to *redeem* man, to buy him back the opportunity of *working out* his true destiny, of earning grace by use of grace, of earning Heaven at the last. In a word, God wanted man to *merit,* and to merit *in justice,* the end He had set for him. Of course, man could not merit existence, he could not merit the first graces, he could not merit an absolute assurance of his own unflinching fidelity and perseverance unto the end; but he could merit graces after the first grace was given, and he could merit right up to the end, *if* he remained faithful to the use of grace, and so could merit Heaven and his last end.

Now, since God wished man to be able to merit grace and Heaven in the way described (and Scripture testifies that He did and does), then the injury wrought towards God by man's sin had to be wiped out, paid for, fully atoned for—otherwise there might be talk of *mercy,* but there could be none of *justice,* for the claims of man. Justice bears an even balance. Restoration in the measure of justice is an equal restoration. A restoration in justice for man's sin must have the *extent* of man's sin; or rather, the price paid for restoration must be as valuable as that which man's sin had taken away.

Now, man's sin was *infinite* in malice; it did an infinite injury to God; it was an affront which was an infinite indignity to God. How, you may say, could poor, finite man commit an infinite offence? Consider: "Injury is in the person injured." The first measure of offence is the person offended. If a soldier in the ranks strikes a fellow-soldier, the offence is not very serious; if the private soldier strikes his lieutenant, the offence is more serious; if the private soldier strikes his general, the offence is still more serious, and so on. Yet the thing done was precisely the same in all cases—a blow struck. The measure of the offence is, first and foremost, in the personage offended; secondarily, it is in the status of the offender, and the lower or more dependent that status, the greater is the offence. Now, sin is an offence against God, whose majesty is infinite, and hence sin is infinite. It is an infinite injury done to God, not indeed that it *hurts* or *maims* the divine substance itself, but that it outrages the divine majesty and dignity. Then sin is done by man, most favored by God, heaped with gifts, given existence, kept in existence, all by the goodness of God. Man is totally dependent upon God. Hence, when man offends God, the offence is ingratitude unspeakable, impertinence unthinkable. So, man's first sin was an infinite offence: infinite in outraging infinite majesty, infinite

in unfathomable ingratitude and impertinence. And,
lastly, the very nature of man's first sin shows that
it was a very serious thing *in itself*. God forbade man
to eat a certain fruit. It was a simple thing, an easy
obedience that was exacted. But God made it plain
that the obligation was not a light one; for He declared that death would follow disobedience, and so
it did, and passed upon all men, so that all must die,
and in the moment of sin our first parents died the
spiritual death, which consists in the loss of that gift
of infinite value, grace.

Sin, then, has an infinite malice or badness. How,
therefore, should finite man atone for it *in justice,*
so that the extent of the offence should be equaled by
the extent of the atonement? You may say, if man
could commit an infinite offence, could he not effect
an infinite work of reparation? No, for just as "injury is in the person injured," so "atonement is in
the work of the *person atoning":* the offence was
measured by the infinite majesty of God; the atonement, in so far as man might offer to make it, would
be measured by the finite capacity of man. Man could
not atone in the measure exacted by justice. Yet man
should atone, for man did the offence. Here, then, is
an *impasse:* man owes an infinite debt and cannot pay
it; God can pay an infinite price, but does not owe it.
Is this the end, then? Is the redemption impossible?
No; for the wisdom and power of God now shine
forth in a work that passes far beyond the wildest

hopes and thoughts of man : God gives a Redeemer
who is *both God and Man:* He is God, and *can* pay
the infinite price of redemption in the measure of justice; He is man, and of the race that *should* pay that
price. God became man in the *Incarnation,* the act by
which the Second Person of the Blessed Trinity, remaining God, remaining a single Person, assumed to
Himself human nature, becoming true man as well as
true God : the Nature of God and the nature of man
being perfectly united in the One undivided Person
of the Son of God. The Incarnation was *necessary,*
given God's will to receive for man's fall an equal
atonement in justice.

There is need of redemption for man ; there is need
of a Redeemer who is both God and Man.

c) THE FACT OF REDEMPTION

That Jesus Christ is both true God and true Man
we shall show in subsequent Chapters. That Christ
is the true Redeemer we shall show in the next Article
of the present Chapter. Here, for the sake of completeness in the study we have immediately in hand,
we merely state the fact of the accomplished Redemption.

Man needs a Redeemer. The Redeemer must be
both God and Man. It is a matter of history as well
as of revelation that the human race expected the
coming of such a redeemer. When the time of expec-

tation was accomplished, the Redeemer came—Jesus Christ was born.

Christ lived for thirty years in almost complete obscurity, and then for three years He was a public figure. He was indeed a Great Teacher, for He taught Truth to men; but the chief work He had to do was to die, to offer His life in sacrifice to God, an infinite price for the infinite debt which man had incurred by sin. G. K. Chesterton says (*The Everlasting Man*, p. 253): "Now . . . the life of Jesus of Nazareth went as swift and as straight as a thunderbolt . . . it did above all things consist in doing something that had to be done. It emphatically would not have been done, if Jesus had walked about the world for ever doing nothing except tell the truth. . . . The primary thing he was going to do was to die. He was going to do other things equally definite and objective . . . but from first to last the most definite fact is that he is going to die."

That Jesus Christ died is a fact of plain history. That He rose again from the dead is equally plain history, although there are some that are not allowed to believe it by their narrow and ugly philosophies, which reject *a priori* anything of a miraculous nature. Still, it is plain history, as we shall see in another Chapter. The results of this death and Resurrection were: the satisfaction of God's *justice* for the sin of man, and the opening of Heaven and the gaining of grace (help to Heaven) for men. This, in very brief, is what is meant by *the fact of Redemption.*

The sufferings and death of Christ (who is *true God* as well as true man) are atoning acts of God, and hence of *infinite value.* Thus they are an infinite price paid for an infinite debt: justice is satisfied. Man has again the opportunity which he lost in the primal sin, viz., the opportunity of achieving the purpose of his being, of attaining of his last end. But, as we have seen, man is crippled in his finest faculties as a result of original sin. Of what use is the opening of Heaven if weakened and injured human nature cannot get there? The Redeemer supplies the lack: He gains grace for men, He founds His Church to be the continual means and fount of grace unto men, and to guide them safely to Heaven. The Redemption, as a matter of fact, is a complete Redemption. Man has his opportunity once more; the accomplishment of his end is in his own hands; effort and good-will (with grace) will achieve it. But, as the whole of humanity stood at trial in the trial of Adam, so now humanity stands at trial in its individual members. As Adam had to choose God or reject Him; so each individual man has now to choose God or reject Him. And he who would choose God must inquire out the *truth* about the meaning of life, must know and practice the *true religion,* must avail himself of the *means of grace.* Thus only can men take advantage of the opportunity purchased for them in the Redemption.

SUMMARY OF THE ARTICLE

In this lengthy Article we have learned the meaning of *redemption,* and have seen that, in view of original sin and its effect, man stands in need of redemption. We have seen that the Redeemer, to satisfy the even demands of *justice* in the work of redemption, must be *man,* and still must be capable of doing a work of infinite value which mere man cannot do: in a word, we have seen that while the Redeemer must be *man,* he must also be *God.* We have outlined the historical events which constitute the Redemption as a fact, and have indicated its results for men.

ARTICLE 2. THE REDEEMER

a) The Promise of a Redeemer   b) The Promise Fulfilled
in Christ

a) THE PROMISE OF A REDEEMER

The promise of a Redeemer was made by Almighty God to our first parents immediately after the Fall. The devil, in the form of a serpent, had brought temptation into the world, and temptation led to sin. But the triumph of the devil was not to be complete; he was to be defeated in the end; he was to be crushed by "the woman and her *seed* (i. e., the Redeemer)." For God said (Genesis iii, 15): "I will put enmities between thee [the serpent] and the woman, and thy seed and her seed: she shall crush thy head, and thou shalt lie in wait for her heel."

The promise of God was explained and amplified by the many utterances of the prophets, who foretold the coming of the Redeemer at various times from eight hundred to four hundred years before His advent, and indicated His personage, character, and work in great detail. Thus, the prophets foretold facts concerning the Redeemer's:

1. *time:* The Redeemer was to come seventy weeks of years (i. e., 490 years) after the Jews returned from the captivity of Babylon (Daniel ix, 24): "Seventy weeks (i. e., of years) are shortened (i. e., fixed and determined) upon thy people, and upon thy holy city, that transgression may be finished, and sin may have an end, and iniquity may be abolished, and everlasting justice may be brought, and vision and prophecy may be fulfilled; and the Saint of saints may be anointed."

2. *birth:* The Redeemer was to be born of a virgin (Isaias vii, 14): "Therefore, the Lord Himself shall give you a sign. Behold, a virgin shall conceive, and bear a son, and His name shall be called Emmanuel."

3. *birthplace:* The Redeemer was to be born in Bethlehem (Micheas v, 2): "And thou, Bethlehem Ephrata, art a little one among the thousands of Juda: out of thee shall come forth unto me that is

to be the ruler in Israel, and his going forth is from the beginning, from the days of eternity." When the Magi came seeking the new-born King of the Jews, Herod summoned the chief priests and scribes and asked them where the Messias was to be born. They answered (Matthew ii, 5) : "In Bethlehem of Juda: for so it is written by the prophet."

4. *name:* The Redeemer was to be the Messias (i. e., The Anointed), Christ (i. e., The Anointed), Jesus (i. e., Savior or Redeemer) (Matthew i, 21) : "Thou shalt call his name Jesus, for he shall save his people from their sins." (Luke ii, 11) : "This day is born to you a Savior, who is Christ the Lord." The Redeemer was also to be called Emmanuel (i. e., God with us), and this name is truly applied to Christ who is true God as well as true man.

5. *lineage:* The Redeemer was to be born of the "house and family of David" (Jeremias xxiii, 5) : "I will raise up to David a just branch." Our Lord asked the Pharisees about the family from which the Messias was to come, saying, "Whose son is he (i. e., Christ)?" They answered Him, "David's."

6. *recognition by kings bearing gifts* (Psalm lxxi, 10) : "The kings of Tharsis and the islands shall offer presents; the kings of the Arabians and of Saba shall bring gifts."

7. *works of mercy* (Isaias xxxv) : "Then shall the eyes of the blind be opened, and the ears of the deaf

shall be unstopped." (Isaias lxi, 1) : ". . . the Lord hath anointed me : he hath sent me to preach to the meek, to heal the contrite of heart . . ."

8. *betrayal* (Zacharias xi, 12) : "And they weighed for my wages thirty pieces of silver." St. Matthew (xxvii, 9) speaks of the return of the thirty pieces of silver by the despairing Judas, and the purchase of a burying ground for strangers with the sum : "Then was fulfilled that which was spoken by the prophet Jeremias, saying : And they took the thirty pieces of silver, the price of him that was prized, whom they prized of the children of Israel : and they gave them unto the potter's field . . ."

9. *sufferings:* The Redeemer was to be *rebuked, struck, spit upon* (Isaias l, 6) : "I have given my body to the strikers, and my cheeks to them that plucked them : I have not turned away my face from them that rebuked me, and spit upon me." The Redeemer was to be crucified (Psalm xxi, 17) : "They have dug my hands and feet."

10. *resurrection:* The Redeemer's grave was not to contain corruption, but was to be *glorious* with life (Isaias xi, 10) : ". . . his sepulchre shall be glorious." (Psalm xv, 10) : ". . . nor wilt thou give thy holy one to see corruption."

11. *ascension* (Psalm lxvii, 19) : "Thou hast ascended on high. . . ."

12. *founding of the Church:* The Redeemer was to establish a kingdom that should have no end (Dan-

iel ii, 44) : ". . . the God of Heaven will set up a kingdom that shall never be destroyed. . . ."

13. *divinity* (Isaias xxxv, 4) : "God Himself will come and will save you."

b) THE PROMISE FULFILLED IN CHRIST

We have given several prophecies concerning the Redeemer. Many others might be added to the list. Still, these are sufficient. And if it be found that all of these prophecies are fulfilled in Jesus Christ, then it is inevitably certain that Jesus Christ is indeed the Messias, the Redeemer. We evidence here the fact that these prophecies are truly fulfilled in Jesus Christ:

1. The time foretold for the coming of the Redeemer in the text quoted from Daniel, and in others connected with the destruction of the Temple of Jerusalem, is the time of Christ's life and death. The whole people was in expectation of the Redeemer at the very time in which Christ was born.

2. Jesus Christ was born of the Virgin Mary. The fact of her spotless virginity is attested by the Gospels. St. Matthew (i, 22) expressly states that the prophecy of Isaias, quoted above, was fulfilled in the virgin birth. St. Joseph, spouse of Mary, knew of her virginity, and was in consternation when he learned that she was to give birth to a child; he was divinely assured that "that which is conceived in her is of the Holy Ghost."

3. Christ was born in Bethlehem, as the prophets had declared the Redeemer would be.

4. Jesus Christ bore the name foretold by the prophets as the name of the Redeemer: He was called Jesus, Christ, Emmanuel.

5. Jesus Christ was "of the house and family of David." Joseph and Mary (being relatives) were both of this kingly house, and repaired to Bethlehem, the city of David, to be enrolled according to the decree of Augustus: while they were there, Christ was born.

6. The Magi, bearing gifts, fulfilled the prophecy which declared that kings should offer presents and bring gifts to the Redeemer.

7. In Acts x, 38 we read that Jesus Christ "went about doing good." The Gospels are full of reports of his deeds of mercy. St. John declares that the recorded mercies of Christ are as nothing compared to their actual number. In special, Christ did many times cure the blind and deaf; he preached to the meek; he forgave sins, thus healing the contrite of heart.

8. The Gospels record the betrayal of Christ for thirty pieces of silver.

9. Jesus Christ was rebuked, struck, spit upon; His hands and feet were pierced or "dug" when He was affixed to the cross.

10. Jesus Christ rose from the dead, glorious and immortal, on the third day after His death. We shall

treat of this crowning miracle in detail when we come to the proof of the divinity of Christ.

11. The Acts of the Apostles (i, 9) tells of the ascension of Christ: "And . . . while they looked on, he was raised up; and a cloud received him out of their sight."

12. That Christ founded His true Church, which shall endure forever, and which is the kingdom of God for men, we shall prove in a later Chapter. Here it will suffice to mention the fact that He sent the Apostles to teach all men the truths of his religion and promised to abide with them forever (Matthew xxviii, 19, 20): "Going therefore, teach ye all nations: baptizing them in the name of the Father, and of the Son, and of the Holy Ghost: teaching them to observe all things whatsoever I have commanded you: and behold I am with you all days, even to the consummation of the world."

13. That Christ was true God we shall show in the next Chapter.

SUMMARY OF THE ARTICLE

In this Article we listed several prophecies made long before the coming of the Redeemer, indicating what and who the Redeemer should be, and what His work should accomplish. Then we verified each of the prophecies in the person and work of Christ. It follows, then, that Christ is the Redeemer foretold by the prophets.

CHAPTER II

JESUS CHRIST, TRUE GOD

This Chapter offers argument in proof of the divinity of Christ. Divinity belongs to God alone, and to show that Christ is divine means simply to show that Christ is God.

The argument proceeds in this fashion: Jesus Christ claimed to be God, and He proved His claim by His personal character, His wondrous works, and by prophecies which were perfectly fulfilled. The Chapter is divided into four Articles, as follows:

Article 1. Jesus Christ claimed to be God

Article 2. Jesus Christ Proved Himself God by His Personal Character

Article 3. Jesus Christ Proved Himself God by His Wondrous Works

Article 4. Jesus Christ Proved Himself God by His Prophecies

ARTICLE 1. JESUS CHRIST CLAIMED TO BE GOD

a) The Claim of Christ   b) The Character of the Claim

a) THE CLAIM OF CHRIST

1. Standing before the High Priest, Jesus Christ claimed to be God (Matthew xxvi, 63, 64): "And the High Priest said to him [i. e., Christ]: I adjure thee by the living God, that thou tell us if thou be Christ, the Son of God. Jesus saith to him: Thou hast said it [i. e., I am]."

2. In claiming equality with God the Father, Jesus Christ claimed to be God. (John v, 19–21) : "For what things soever he [the Father] doth, these the Son doth also in like manner. . . . For as the Father raiseth up the dead, and giveth life; so the Son also giveth life to whom he will." In His prayer to the Father, Christ also claimed this equality. (John xvii, 10) : "All my things are thine, and thine are mine."

3. In claiming to be one with the Father, Jesus Christ claimed to be God. (John x, 30) : "I and the Father are one." (John x, 38) : "Believe that the Father is in me, and I in the Father." (John xiv, 9, 10) : "Philip, he that seeth me, seeth the Father also. How sayest thou: Show us the Father? Do you not believe that I am in the Father and the Father in me?"

4. In commending the Apostles for confessing Him as God, Jesus Christ claimed to be God. (Matthew xvi, 13–17) : "And Jesus came into the quarters of Cæsarea Philippi: and he asked his disciples, saying: Who do men say that the Son of man is? But they said: Some John the Baptist, and other some Elias, and others Jeremias, or one of the prophets. Jesus saith to them: But who do you say that I am? Simon Peter answered, and said: Thou art Christ, the Son of the living God. And Jesus answering, said to him: Blessed art thou, Simon Bar-Jona: because flesh and blood hath not revealed it to thee, but my Father who is in heaven."

5. In claiming to be the supreme lawgiver, Jesus

Christ claimed to be God. (Matthew xii, 8) : "For the Son of man is Lord, even of the Sabbath." That is: I am God; it is I who have made the Sabbath a day of special observance in my own honor; I, therefore, can set aside that observance if I choose. (Matthew v, 21, 22) : "You have heard that it was said to them of old: Thou shalt not kill: and whosoever shall kill, shall be in danger of the judgment. But *I* say to you: that whosoever is angry with his brother, shall be in danger of the judgment. . . ." That is: I am God, and I can thus explain and amplify the application of the divine law.

6. In claiming to be the supreme judge of men, Jesus Christ claimed to be God. (Matthew xxv, 31, 32) : "And when the Son of man shall come in his majesty, and all the Angels with him, then shall he sit upon the seat of his majesty: and all nations shall be gathered together before him, and he shall separate them one from another, as the shepherd separateth the sheep from the goats." Again, in the judgment Christ shall say (Matthew xxv, 34–40) : "Come, ye blessed . . . possess the kingdom . . . for *I* was hungry and you gave *me* to eat, *I* was thirsty and you gave *me* to drink . . . etc. Then shall the just answer him, saying: Lord, when did we see thee hungry and feed thee, thirsty and we gave thee to drink . . . ? And the king [Christ] answering, shall say to them: Amen, I say to you, as long as you did it to one of these, my least brethren, you did it to *me*."

That is: I, your judge, deem as done to me the deeds of mercy done to my brethren: I, your God, deem as done to me the kindnesses done to my human creatures. The citation continues with the condemnation of those who have not shown mercy to their fellowmen, and their neglect of this duty is mentioned as neglect of the judge, Christ, and as neglect of *God,* since it merits banishment from Heaven.

7. In claiming the accepting *adoration,* which is due to God alone, Jesus Christ claimed to be God. To the man born blind whom He had restored to sight, He said (John ix, 35 ff.) : "Dost thou believe in the Son of God? He answered, and said: Who is he, Lord, that I may believe in him? And Jesus said to him: . . . it is he that talketh with thee. And he said: I believe, Lord. And falling down, he adored him." Again, when Our Lord came to the Apostles, walking upon the water (Matthew xiv, 33) : "They that were in the boat came and adored him, saying: Indeed thou art the Son of God."

8. In claiming and exercising the power to forgive sins *by his own authority* and without having this authority communicated to him, Jesus Christ claimed to be God. (Mark ii, 5) : "Son, thy sins are forgiven thee." (Luke vii, 48) : "And he said to her: Thy sins are forgiven thee." When Christ cured the man sick of the palsy, he worked a miracle in proof that "the Son of man hath power on earth to forgive sins."

9. The Apostles understood the claim of Christ to be God, and willingly suffered and died in testimony of its truth. See the *Acts of the Apostles* iii, 14, 15; v, 41; vii, 56–58; viii, 37; xv, 26; xx, 28.

10. In claiming to be eternal and in using as His own the very name of God (i. e., "I am who am"), Jesus Christ claimed to be God. (John viii, 58) : "Before Abraham was made, I am."

b) THE CHARACTER OF THE CLAIM

The claim of Christ to be God was a literal claim, a real claim. It is not to be explained by being explained away. Christ did not use figurative language when He made this claim, nor did He mean anything less than just what He claimed : He *claimed to be God*.

In claiming to be "the Son of God," Christ claimed to be God. It is true that, in one sense, every man may call himself a child or son of God; it was, indeed, the pride and boast of the Hebrews of Christ's time that they were the favored people of God, and they delighted to call themselves "sons of God." But Christ did not make merely this common claim, nor did the Jews understand Him as making a common claim. The Jews would not have resented such a common claim, but they did resent Christ's claim; they were enraged at it, and uttered a great cry against His blasphemy, and rent their garments in fury. They clamored for the death of Christ and said (John xix, 7) : "He ought to die, because he made himself the

Son of God." They mocked Christ on the Cross, and said (Matthew xxvii, 40): "Vah, . . . if thou be the Son of God, come down from the cross." There can be no doubt whatever that Christ, in calling Himself the Son of God, claimed to be God in very truth.

Let us investigate the meaning of the claim of Christ, following out each item of the first section of this Article:

1. The High Priest adjured Christ by the living God that He tell them whether He was in truth the Son of God, i. e., God Himself. Christ answered simply that He was. That the High Priest understood the full import of the claim is evident from what followed (Matthew xxvi, 65, 66): "Then the High Priest rent his garments, saying: He hath blasphemed, what further need have we of witnesses? Behold, now you have heard the blasphemy: what think you? But they answering, said: He is guilty of death."

2. The claim to be equal with the Father is the claim to be God. God is infinite and indivisible, and can have no equal other than Himself. Hence, the claim to be equal with the Father is the claim to be one with the Father; in other words, it is the claim to *be* the indivisible God.

3. The claim "I and the Father are one" is also the claim to be God. That the Jews understood the claim so, and resented it, is evident from the verse of Scripture which follows that which records the

claim (John x, 31) : "The Jews then took up stones to throw at him."

4. It is evident from the solemnity of St. Peter's confession, "Thou art Christ, the Son of the living God," that the title "Son of God" was no ordinary title to be applied to any man or to any Jew. It was a real confession of the divinity of Christ. And Christ declared that God had made known to Peter this great truth, viz., the truth of His divinity. This was an indubitable claim on the part of Christ that He is truly God.

5. God alone can be the authoritative interpreter of divine laws, unless, indeed, He imparts this office to others. But Christ claims no imparted authority, but explains the extent of the Third and Fifth Commandments "as one having authority."

6. It is the task of God to judge all men. God creates all, preserves all, sets the end for all to achieve. It is inconceivable that any other than God should, of himself, have the right to judge mankind. Yet Christ claims such a right. Therefore, Christ claims to be God.

7. Christ claimed and accepted adoration. And it was Christ Himself who said that adoration was to be given only to God (Matthew iv, 10) : "The Lord thy *God* shalt thou adore." Therefore, in claiming the adoration which is due to God alone, Christ claimed to be God.

8. Christ forgave sins, not as the priests of His Church do, i. e., by authority communicated to them by God. The priests of God's Church really do forgive sin; they do not merely declare it forgiven. But their power to forgive sin is *received* in their ordination, and comes down to them through the long succession of bishops who are the successors of the Apostles, to whom Christ committed the power. Christ forgave sins by His own power, a power *not received;* for He never stated that His power was communicated to Him. Besides, only God can commission men and clothe them with the power to forgive sins, and Christ commissioned His Apostles and clothed them and their successors (and the priests ordained by them and their successors) with the power to forgive sins. Hence, Christ claimed the power of God, and therefore claimed to be God.

9. This point is self-explanatory. Read the citations given.

10. In the Book of Exodus (iii, 14) we read that God called Himself "I am whom am," and when Moses asked God how he should show the Israelites that God had sent him to lead them out of bondage, God said, "I am who am. He said: Thus shalt thou say to the children of Israel: *He who is* hath sent me to you." By using this name, "I am," and by claiming eternity, Christ claimed to be very God.

In this Article we have studied abundant evidence that Christ claimed to be God, and that this claim is not capable of being interpreted in any metaphorical sense, but is a literal and true claim.

In passing, we may mention that Harnack, the great German rationalist (1851–1930), admits that the Gospels are historical documents, and that they show a true claim of Christ to be God. Harnack was a bitter opponent of the truth of Christ's divinity, but the point is that he admits the fact that the claim was made. (Cf. *Lukas der Arzt,* p. 118).

ARTICLE 2. JESUS CHRIST PROVED HIMSELF GOD BY HIS PERSONAL CHARACTER

a) The Public Appearance of Christ   b) The Virtues of Christ   c) The Teaching of Christ

a) THE PUBLIC APPEARANCE OF CHRIST

Out of Nazareth, a poor and backward village of Galilee, there came a Man who stood suddenly before the world and spoke as never man had spoken before. Thirty years earlier He was born at Bethlehem, and the Jewish world was startled by wild tales of shepherds about singing angels and the birth of the Savior. Strange figures appeared in the streets of Jerusalem, and royal trains moved forward to find a new-born King beneath His star. And then the land was filled with wild and passionate mourning for little children slaughtered in His name. Silence came then, and forgetfulness. Once, twelve years after the stirring events of His first coming, the Boy was seen in the Capital, where He confronted the solemn doctors and savants in the Temple and filled their minds with a strange wonder and their hearts with a new humility. Again came mysterious silence until, at the age of thirty, Christ appeared publicly among men. From being the most obscure of private personages He became at once the most notable of public figures, the most admired, the most beloved, the most sought after, the most hated, the most shunned, the most feared.

About this Christ, new come before the people's eyes, strange rumors were abroad from the first: that He claimed to be the Messias foretold of the prophets; that He spoke familiarly of God as His Father in a way in which no other man dared speak; that He called Himself the *Son of man,* as the Scriptures had called the Messias; that He claimed to be older than Abraham, long centuries silent in his grave; that He claimed to be one with God; that He declared He was God Himself.

The people cried, "Is not this the carpenter's son?" And yet, following an impulse of their hearts which they were too earnest and eager to analyze or question, they followed Him and hung upon His words. Homes, money, work, food, comfort—all were forgotten if only they might be with Christ and hear Him speak. Their acknowledgment of Christ's marvellous eloquence, power, and attractiveness was a submission, even though unwilling, of their hearts and wills to the claims of the Messias. Christ appeared among men; people wondered, were resentful, were ready to scoff, but, in spite of themselves, they became His followers.

The proud citizens of the larger cities, looking (with the scorn that we all recognize as a weakness of residents of big communities) upon the upstart leader from the rural districts, sneered and said, "Doth the Christ come out of Galilee?" And yet the townspeople flocked to hear Him, to wonder at His works, to implore His help. Countryfolk and townspeople alike were forced to admit that "never did man speak like this man." And they returned home from His presence, murmuring in an almost half-witted amazement, "We have seen wonderful things to-day." In spite of themselves, men acknowledged Jesus Christ as the Messias sent of God. His appearance among men marked the beginning of His sway over human hearts and wills, and is itself a proof of the fact that Christ is more than man.

The Pharisees railed against Jesus; they planned and they plotted. Forgetting their pride, they were moved at the last to match their trained wits with this untaught Villager. They left the encounter humbled and confounded. Their wisest schemes went for nothing; their craftiest plots were made to look silly; their deep scheming was turned against them for their own confusion. Soon they learned that it was a dangerous business to meddle with Him, and they dared not "ask Him any more questions." The Pharisees and the Scribes and the Ancients of the people hated Christ, but they could not ignore Him; they despised Him, but they could not forget Him. The very appearance of Christ among men marks Him as the centre of things. Love and hatred were thenceforth to swirl about Him; but nevermore was He to be the object of a general indifference. Again, His very appearance marked Christ as more than a mere man.

Stories of the meekness of Christ were told: of His doctrine of turning the other cheek, and forgiving an enemy seventy times seven offences. Jewish hearts were saddened to think upon the ancient military glory of their people, of the warlike manliness of the great Machabeus, and the long line of fighting men that foreshadowed the Messias, back to the towering Saul, whose mighty spear was sung in legend, and the arm of David that alone was strong enough to wield the sword of the fallen giant of the Philistines. And the new Leader was meek and mild! Swarthy faces were alight with unholy laughter; and yet the laughter had scarcely died upon their lips, when news was brought of the meek Christ turning with overpowering anger upon the traffickers in the holy place and sweeping them all before Him down the Temple steps. Tales were told of the gentleness of Christ, and sinewy giants smiled scornfully in their beards; but the smile was frozen in astonishment as word was brought of how Christ had confronted the exalted leaders of the people in the public streets, and told them they were hypocrites and serpents, and asked them with a kind of quiet fury how they hoped to escape damnation. The appearance of Christ among men was as no other appearance had ever been. What strange new contradiction was this that combined meekness with power, and gentleness with masterful authority? As startling and as unmistakable as the new star that came with His birth was the coming of Christ, the Savior, among men.

In a word, never did a more astounding, a more seemingly contradictory fact confront the world than the fact of Jesus Christ. Never did a more command- ing figure meet the eyes of men than the Figure that appeared so suddenly out of Galilee to make a claim upon minds and hearts that was as stupendous as it was irrefutable. Christ appeared; never since that moment has He disappeared. The world loves or hates Him, but in all the long ages and all the races of men, wherever His name has been named and His claim made known, He has remained forever.

Other men have made large claims upon the love and loyalty of men or upon their hatred. They have made their claims, and their claims have all been forgotten. Apollonius of Tyana claimed a sort of limited divinity, and he backed up his claim with some first-rate trickery; but not one man in ten knows to-day who Apollonius of Tyana was, or when or where he lived. Socrates, Plato, and Aristotle share among them the high honor that is vaguely paid to what is still more vaguely known as "the learning of the ancient Greeks." But comparatively few among modern men know what these learned philosophers taught, and fewer care. They are revered for their intellect wherever weak men worship intellect, but they are not loved or hated as Christ is loved or hated. Mohammed appeared among men, much later than Christ, and claimed an intimacy with God that was both startling and engaging. He built up a following that endures to this day. But the most ardent Mohammedan does not regard the "Prophet" as God, nor does he love him with anything like the passion and personal directness with which he hates Jesus Christ. The very hatred of the Mohammedan is a confession that Christ is a nearer presence, a truer reality, than the sole high-exalted prophet of Allah: nay, Christ is to him a reality more intimate than Allah himself. Confucius taught a philosophy which modern stupidity persists in regarding as a religion; but the world to-day looks upon Confucius with the mere detached and unenthusiastic approval with which it regards Seneca or Marcus Aurelius. Christ alone of all men that ever walked the earth is at the very centre of human life. Around Him alone rises the deathless cry of battle, the cry of attack and of defence, which marks Him as the one personage in whom all men have ever a passionate interest. Around Christ, and around Christ alone, surge the tides of human love and loyalty and the tides of human bitterness and hatred: He stands at the centre forever, immovable, unforgettable. And so it has been since His strange and sudden appearance among men when He came, emaciated and weak from His long fasting, to bring to mankind the "good news" for which the patriarchs had sighed.

The appearance of Christ among men, and the facts that came with that appearance—facts that have remained in the expanse of human history like fixed stars in the wide sweep of the sky—mark Christ as *unique* among men, as the one and only Man of his kind, as *more* than man. The appearance of Christ, and the facts that came with that appearance, are proof enough for any mind that ever functioned in the simplest thought, that Jesus Christ *is very God*. It is not the Crucifixion and its wonders that is needed, it is not even the glorious and all-sufficing Resurrection that is required, to convince sound and honest reason of the fact that "indeed this *is* the Son of God." The appearance of Christ is the appearance of a fact that has never been destroyed, although a thousand times contradicted and denied. That appearance is itself a proof,

positive and irrefutable, that God has indeed "be·
come flesh and pitched his tent among us."

b) THE VIRTUES OF CHRIST

In perfect innocence or sinlessness, as well as in
positive virtues, Christ is the crowning glory of the
human race. The world has not lacked its giants of
heroic virtue, nor has it been without its ideals of
perfection. But Christ not only rises superior to all
the heroes and the saints; He surpasses all their
ideals as well. He not only surpasses the achieve-
ments of other men; He surpasses their finest thoughts
of what is achievable.

The friends of Christ declare that He is "un-
spotted," "undefiled," "the just," "the one in whom
there is no sin." The enemies of Christ bear the self-
same testimony to His stainless glory. Judas, who
betrayed Him, said He was innocent; Pilate, who
condemned Him, could find "no cause" in Him, and
said He was a just man! the Pharisees, who watched
His every movement and gesture and listened eagerly
for a careless word that might serve them "to entrap
Him in His speech," could bring but one true charge
against Him when He stood at trial, and that was that
He claimed to be God—which was only the claim to
be recognized for what He really is.

Nor was Christ merely without sin; He possessed
the fulness of positive virtue. His charity (love) was

perfect, and He summed up the whole duty of man in the twofold commandment of love of God and neighbor. His zeal for the honor of God was boundless, and, while He rebuked those that gave mere outward observance to the law of the Sabbath, He furiously drove before Him the men that desecrated the holy place. His eagerness for the fulfilment of God's will extended even to the dark hour of agony. His anxiety for the welfare of souls made Him preach and threaten and pray, and brought tears to His eyes when He looked upon the unresponsive city. His quickness to forgive sin was evident wherever the smallest spark of repentance showed itself. His obedience to His Mother and to his Guardian, His mercy to the poor and sinful, His kindness to the sick and the bereaved and those possessed of devils, His unswerving justice, His hatred of sin combined with love for the sinner—these and a hundred more detailed virtues marked Christ as immeasurably the greatest moral character that the world has ever known. We need no confirmation of this fact in human words: we need only look at the impression Christ has left upon human minds through two thousand years. Yet if we needed words, they are not wanting; nor shall we take them from the lips of Christians. Rousseau declares that no hero of history is comparable with Christ, and he says of those who venerate the character of Socrates as the ideal of human achievement, "How blind must one be that dares compare the son of Sophroniscus with the Son of Mary!" Lecky, a rationalist, says: "It was reserved for Christianity to present to the world an ideal character, which through all the changes of eighteen centuries has inspired the hearts of men with an impassioned love; has shown itself capable of acting on all ages, nations, temperaments, and conditions; has been not only the highest pattern of virtue, but the strongest incentive to its practice, and has exercised so deep an influence that it may be truly said that the simple record of three short years of active life has done more to regenerate and soften mankind, than all the disquisitions of philosophers, and all the exhortations of moralists." (Quoted from *History of European Morals,* Vol. II, p. 8, by Most Rev. M. Sheehan in *Apologetics and Catholic Doctrine,* Part I, p. 59.) Harnack, who denies the divinity of Christ, finds Him a figure of incomparable virtue and holiness and a teacher of fathomless wisdom.

Now, the fact that Christ was a model of innocence and virtue is not *in itself* a proof that He is God. But it *is* a proof that He is not a deceiver; it *is* a proof that Christ could not have lied when He claimed that He was God. Thus, indirectly, Christ's superhuman virtue and innocence prove Him to be God.

Indeed, the rationalists who deny the divinity of Christ have no reason to admire His virtues at all. For if Christ is not divine, then He has made a false claim, and has deceived millions of souls for hundreds of years. Surely, if we do not admit that Christ is God, we cannot admit that Christ is good. Nay, we are justified in declaring with G. K. Chesterton, "Really, if Jesus of Nazareth was not Christ (i. e., *the* Christ, the Messias, God), He must have been Antichrist."

One who makes claim to be God must be doing one of three things. He must be following a single mad idea as a maniac; or he must be making a stupendous effort to deceive all men; or he must be simply telling the truth. Now, no one has ever seriously contended that Christ was mad; the balance of His life, the balance of His profound reasoning, the moderation and justice of His words and deeds, destroy that assumption as with a blast of annihilation. Nor could such a man as Christ have been a mere deceiver; the marvellous virtues admitted on all hands as His, and His alone, make the thought impossible. It remains that Christ, claiming to be God, was simply telling the truth.

Thus does the perfection of the character of Christ, thus do His innocence and virtues, show Him unmistakably to be very God.

c) THE TEACHING OF CHRIST

The personal character of Christ as the most perfect *teacher* the world has ever known, or, before His coming, even believed possible, is a further proof of His more than human character. Even though Our

Lord came first and foremost *to die,* He came also to teach. He left the task of teaching largely to His Apostles and His Church, commissioning and instructing these agencies through His own word and the Holy Ghost, whom He sent upon them. But Christ certainly taught, and as a teacher of religion He stands unequaled among all the great teachers of men.

Now, the characteristics of a great teacher are these: he must have great knowledge and he must impart it with power and effect. The sublimity of the doctrine taught by Christ, the perfection of the knowledge He displayed, and the tremendous force and influence of His teaching mark Him as the greatest teacher of all times.

The body of doctrine taught by Our Lord needs no detailed mention here. It will be sufficient for the purpose of Apologetics to mention a few of the important items of that teaching.

1. Christ instructed men in the truths that concern God and His perfection, and this in no abstruse style, as one might expect from the greatness of the subject, but in a direct and simple fashion illuminated with striking parables. The least gifted of His hearers could not have failed to understand Christ's teaching, nor could the most learned and gifted of philosophers exhaust the rich content of His doctrine. Time after time Christ began His instruction about God with the words, "The kingdom of heaven

is like to . . . ," and then continued with an exposition of the justice, the mercy, and the providence of God, of His concern for poor mankind, of His requirements in the way of mutual love and justice among men. God was thus brought near to the people. The great *Jehovah* (or *Yahweh*) had been truly worshipped in the manner established by Moses, who was divinely instructed; but He had been far off, even in the Holy of Holies, and, in spite of His countless favors to the Jewish people, He had not been known with that intimate love and trust with which Christ taught people to know Him.

2. Christ taught men the value of their souls, showing them the flowers of the field and the birds of the air, and telling them how valuable they were in comparison with these frail and beautiful things. He showed men that the soul has a value beyond all worldly riches; He pointed to the wealthy Dives and Lazarus, the beggar; He asked men with piercing directness what good it would do to possess the world and then lose their souls.

3. Christ taught men the necessity of reposing trust in God; He taught them to have faith and sincerity in their hearts and souls. He taught, as an essential thing, the love of the poor, and detachment from the slavish pursuit of riches. He taught men to forgive "their brother from their hearts," to preserve themselves clean of heart, to keep themselves pure not only of foul deeds, but of lustful desires, and

declared that the horrible sin of adultery was committed in thought as in deed.

In His teaching Christ spoke, as the people testified, in a manner wholly new to men: "Never did man speak like this man." And not only was His doctrine so complete and perfect as to shame the best efforts of merely human teachers, philosophers, and moralists; it carried a power that men had never experienced before: "He was teaching them as one having power, and not as the Scribes"; "And they were astonished at His doctrine, for His speech was with power." The power of Christ's teaching appears in the fact that men listened to him, "felt their hearts glow within them," followed His teaching, found happiness in following it as nowhere else, and literally transformed the face of the earth, as the great army of Christians began their march through history.

The fact that Christ is the greatest teacher men have known is not, in itself, a proof that He is God. But it *is* a proof that His teaching was most notable and worth while: and the core and centre of that teaching is that He Himself is God! If Christ is acknowledged as a great teacher—and all men do acknowledge Him so—then He must be a true teacher, for a teacher of lies is not great. Christ is a great teacher precisely because He is a true and powerful teacher, precisely because He teaches *truths;* and the greatest truth He teaches is that He is God. Thus does the teaching of Christ proclaim Him to be true God.

Suppose for one instant that Christ was merely vainglorious, that He liked to hold sway over human minds, that He made claim to be God and taught as God from motives of human weakness and vanity. Consider: Could He be desirous of the mere praise of a people that He knew, and accurately foretold, to be His persecutors and murderers? What had He to expect from teaching vanities and deceptions? The whole notion is absurd and impossible.

Those who admire Christ as a teacher, and yet deny His divinity, are utterly unreasonable. For he is not worthy of admiration who perpetrates a stupendous fraud, no matter how superb is his presentation of his false claim. To sane minds the teaching of Christ must bring belief with admiration, for it is folly to profess admiration for Christ's teaching, and yet to consider it false and futile.

SUMMARY OF THE ARTICLE

In this Article we have seen that the personal character of Christ as a public figure, as a being of matchless virtue, and as a teacher, gives infallible evidence that His claim to be God is a true claim.

We have made no appeal to sentiment; we have dealt with the whole matter in a coldly scientific and rational way. Our conclusion is inevitable, and the mind that refuses assent to such evidence as we have here produced can hardly be an honest mind.

ARTICLE 3. JESUS CHRIST PROVED HIMSELF GOD BY HIS WONDROUS WORKS

a) The Miracles of Christ   b) The Resurrection of Christ

a) THE MIRACLES OF CHRIST

Miracles, as we have seen, are marvellous works, out of the ordinary course of nature, and produced by Almighty God. If the marvellous events can be known, then we can recognize them as historical happenings, and we say that we have knowledge of their *historical truth.* If the marvellous works can be known as truly beyond the power of natural causes to produce and as really produced by God, then we can recognize the miracles *as such,* and we say that we have knowledge of their *philosophical truth.* When both the historical and philosophical truth of miracles is established, then we are forced by reason to say: "The finger of God is here"; we are compelled to admit that God approves the doctrine in proof of which a miracle is worked; we are inescapably convinced that miracles are a proof of divine approval.

Now, Christ wrought true miracles. Therefore, the doctrine in proof of which He wrought them is approved of God. But Christ's doctrine concerns two things above all else, viz., His character as true God, and His mission as man's Redeemer. Therefore, the miracles of Christ show unmistakably that God approves as true His claim to be God and man's Redeemer.

The Gospels mention many works of Christ which are unquestionably true miracles. He changed water into wine by the mere act of His will, He fed thousands with a few loaves and fishes, He walked upon water as upon dry land, He stilled the surging sea with a word, He healed the sick instantaneously, He gave sight to the blind and hearing to the deaf, He expelled evil spirits from the afflicted, He raised up the dead to life.

The miracles of Christ cannot be questioned on the score of their *historical* truth. Christ performed them in public, sometimes before hundreds, sometimes before thousands. Nor were these witnesses all friends of Christ; many of them would have liked nothing better than the opportunity of saying that Christ played tricks and wrought no true miracles. But even His enemies did not deny the power or the miracles of Christ. In His trial the accusers did not allege any fraud in His works. They knew that He had raised Lazarus, four days dead, to life again; they did not try to deny this fact, but only plotted to kill Christ, lest the greatness of the miracle draw "the whole world" after Him. His enemies said that Christ cast out devils by the prince of devils, but they did not deny that He cast the devils out. Nor can we suppose

that the great numbers of witnesses to Christ's miracles were merely deluded, that they were credulous
and gullible folk who only thought they saw wonders
wrought. If anyone thinks that the Jewish people
were dull-witted, and credulous, and likely to be mistaken about a thousand miracles performed publicly
and in widely various ways, then he is himself deluded about some of the most patent facts of human
history. If any modern thinks that the watchful Pharisees were deluded by Christ, then the modern is sadly
deluded about the Pharisees. Even from what we
know of the Jew of to-day—and he is singularly like
his forefathers, perhaps more so than any other
man of modern times—we understand that the public
which beheld the miracles of Christ was neither overcredulous nor slow of mind. If we should adhere to
the absurd *delusion theory,* we should be forced to
the conclusion that the Jews of Christ's time were
mere morons and imbeciles. In spite of the impossibility of this theory, it may be well for us to pause
upon it for a little consideration. We shall select for
special study two of the miracles of Christ, viz.,
the raising of Lazarus, and the curing of the man
born blind.

1. The raising of Lazarus (John xi) is a marvellous fact of indubitable historical truth. Lazarus lay
sick at his home in Bethany. His sisters, Mary and
Martha, sent for Christ, who had often visited their
house and who was loved as their dearest friend, and

they were confident that He would come and cure
their brother. But Christ purposely delayed His coming, and did not set out for Bethany until Lazarus
had died, and He knew, and told His disciples, of
the death. When He arrived in Bethany, Lazarus had
been buried for four days. Now—as we learn from
the fact that he had to be "loosed" before he could
walk unhampered—Lazarus had been buried in the
Jewish manner, with the body closely wrapped in
bands, with the face swathed tightly. Even if Lazarus
were not dead when he was placed in the tomb, he
must certainly have suffocated long before the lapse
of four days. There were many with Christ when He
came to the tomb, for we read that after the miracle,
"Many of the Jews who were come to Mary and
Martha and had seen the things that Jesus did, believed in him. But *some* of them, etc. . . ." Then, before many witnesses, in open day, He called upon the
dead man, and Lazarus arose and came forth. There
was certainly no delusion in this miracle. The people saw it; the Pharisees admitted it; the chief priests
did not doubt it; the High Priest never questioned it.
But priests and Pharisees "from that day . . . de-
vised to put him [Christ] to death," lest the greatness
of the miracle should make all believe in Him. If we
can doubt the reality of this miracle we can doubt
the existence of America or the fact of the French
Revolution. If this miracle is not justified historically,
there is no value in human history at all.

2. The cure of the man born blind, as narrated in the Gospel of St. John (ix), is a certain historical fact. Let us quote the charmingly direct and simple account of it as it stands in Scripture: "And Jesus, passing by, saw a man who was blind from his birth. . . . He spat on the ground and made clay of the spittle, and spread the clay upon his eyes, and said to him: Go, wash in the pool of Siloe. He went, therefore, and washed, and came seeing. The neighbors . . . said: Is not this he that sat and begged? Some said: This is he. But others said: No, but he is like him. But he said: I am he. They said therefore to him: How were thy eyes opened? He answered: That man that is called Jesus made clay, and anointed my eyes, and said to me: Go to the pool of Siloe and wash. And I went, I washed, and I see. And they said to him: Where is he? He saith: I know not. They bring him that had been blind to the Pharisees. Now it was the Sabbath when Jesus made the clay and opened his eyes. Again therefore the Pharisees asked him how he had received his sight. But he said to them: He put clay upon my eyes, and I washed, and I see. Some therefore of the Pharisees said: This man is not of God, who keepeth not the Sabbath. But others said: How can a man that is a sinner do such miracles? And there was a division among them. They say therefore to the blind man again: What sayest thou of him that opened thy eyes? And he said: He is a prophet. The Jews then did not believe concerning him that he

had been blind and had received his sight, until they
called the parents of him that had received his sight,
and asked them, saying: Is this your son, who you say
was born blind? How then does he now see? His parents answered them and said: We know that he is
our son and that he was born blind: but how he now
seeth we know not: or who hath opened his eyes we
know not: ask himself; he is of age, let him speak
for himself. These things his parents said because
they feared the Jews, for the Jews had already agreed
among themselves that if any man should confess him
to be Christ, he should be put out of the synagogue.
Therefore did his parents say: He is of age, ask him.
They therefore called the man again that had been
born blind, and said to him: Give glory to God; we
know that this man is a sinner. He said therefore to
them: If he be a sinner, I know not: one thing I know,
that whereas I was blind, I now see. They said then
to him: What did he do to thee? How did he open
thy eyes? He answered them: I have told you already,
and you have heard: why would you hear it again?
Will you also become his disciples? They reviled him
therefore and said: Be thou his disciple; but we are
the disciples of Moses. We know that God spoke
to Moses: but as to this man, we know not from
whence he is. The man answered and said to them:
Why, herein is a wonderful thing that you know not
from whence he is, and he hath opened my eyes. Now
we know that God does not hear sinners; but if a

man be a server of God and doth his will, him he heareth. From the beginning of the world it hath not been heard that any man hath opened the eyes of one born blind. Unless this man were of God he could not do anything. They answered and said to him: Thou wast wholly born in sins, and dost thou teach us? And they cast him out. Jesus heard that they had cast him out: and when he had found him, he said to him: Dost thou believe in the Son of God? He answered and said: Who is he, Lord, that I may believe in him? And Jesus said to him: Thou hast both seen him, and it is he that talketh with thee. And he said: I believe, Lord. And falling down, he adored him."

Notice that the man born blind was unmistakably identified. Notice further that not one among the neighbors, or among the Pharisees, even thought of doubting the miracle as a fact, as a marvellous happening. The miracle was wrought publicly, and with ceremony (for Christ made clay and anointed the man's eyes and directed him to wash in a certain pool), and it seems that the ceremony was meant, at least partly, to call attention to the *fact* of the miracle. There can be no doubt whatever about the historical truth of this miracle.

Christ, then, wrought marvellous events that are known as such. Now what of the *philosophical* truth of these marvels? Can they be known to exceed the powers of nature and to be the work of Almighty God? We assert that they can.

1. The raising of the dead to life is surely not within the powers of created nature. It cannot be the result of any "hidden power or law of nature." To attempt such an explanation is merely to perform an "artful dodge,"—a favorite gesture of those whose ugly theory of things does not allow them to believe in miracles or even to admit that evidence can be offered for their existence. There can be no hidden power of nature that works in a manner contrary to the course of nature : nature is consistent and not self-contradictory; and the very name "nature" is but the general term used to designate the *regular, uniform,* and *constant* course of activity observed in the world. Nature may be said to give life; but nature never gives life to a corpse. Our knowledge of nature and of nature-processes would have to be totally abandoned as so much falsity and futility, natural science would have to be destroyed, the laboratories of the biologist, zoologist, and botanist would have to be abandoned as useless, if nature could restore life once life has become extinct. Besides, even if nature could restore life, which it certainly cannot, the raising of a dead man *at a word* would still be a miracle. If nature had a hidden power within itself which brought Lazarus from death to life, why was that power exercised only when Christ called Lazarus to come forth? And why has it not been exercised in

other instances without the word of God's messenger? We are forced by cold reason to conclude that the raising of the dead is not only a marvellous event, but that it is a marvellous event beyond the power of created nature to produce. Now, was it produced by Almighty God? Christ claimed to be God, and He worked this wonder, by reason of which "many of the Jews . . . believed in him." Besides, the work was one of goodness and kindness; its effect was one that brought men's minds to God and their hearts to submit unto His Law. Certainly, then, the work was of God. "By their fruits you shall know them," is the practical test of the origin of any matter. We conclude that the raising of Lazarus is verified as a true miracle on both points of its *philosophical* character: it was an event outside the power of nature to produce, and it was produced by the power of Almighty God. It was, in plain terms, *a true miracle.* Therefore, it is an unmistakable and incontrovertible evidence that Christ is of God, and that His doctrine is true. Now, the doctrine of Christ is that He is God. Therefore, Christ is God.

2. The giving of sight to a man born blind is a true miracle. The fact that the man cured by Christ was *born* blind, is an evidence that no nervous disorder, no hypochondria, no auto-suggestion, had induced a merely temporary state of irregularity in the man's vision that strong faith or suddenly aroused hope might dispel. Indeed, the man did not know who

Christ was when he felt the clay being placed upon his eyes and was ordered to the pool of Siloe. He was asked about Our Lord later, and responded vaguely that he thought Christ was at least "a prophet." Only when Our Lord found him, after his ejection from the synagogue, was he given the gift of faith; only then did he learn to say, "I believe, Lord." Now, no hidden power of nature can account for this restoration of vision which we consider here. If it could, why did it wait until the ceremony of anointing and washing was performed? Why did it wait for the orders of Christ before it functioned? Why did it function then? In this, as in the raising of Lazarus, we have not only historical truth of a strange event, a marvellous event; we have the philosophical truth of the event as *a miracle,* for it is obviously outside the ordinary course of nature, and was produced (as the character of Christ, the character of the event, and the fruits of the work show) by the power of Almighty God. Now this miracle was wrought to support the claim of Christ to be God, as we see from Christ's words to the man who was cured. Therefore, Christ's claim is true. In a word, Christ is God.

From the two miracles that we have chosen out of the many performed by Christ, we perceive that these marvellous works of Our Lord can be known as true miracles, historically and philosophically, and that the *delusion theory,* which attempts to explain Christ's miracles by explaining them away, is sheer nonsense.

Omitting detailed mention or study of the many other miracles of Our Lord, we come, in the following section, to discuss the crowning miracle of all, viz., the Resurrection of Christ from the dead.

b) THE RESURRECTION OF CHRIST

The Resurrection of Jesus Christ, by His own power, from the dead, is the crowning miracle of His career. Indeed, it is more than a miracle; it is the fulfilment of a prophecy. In St. Matthew (xvii, 9) we read that, after the Transfiguration, Christ said to the three Apostles who had beheld His glory, "Tell the vision to no man till the Son of man *be risen from the dead.*" And in St. John (iii, 19) we read that Our Lord said to the Jews, "Destroy this temple, and in three days I will raise it up. . . . He spoke of the temple of his body." Again, in St. Matthew (xx, 18, 19) we read these words of Christ to His followers, "Behold, we go up to Jerusalem, and the Son of man shall be betrayed to the chief priests and the scribes, and they shall condemn him to death, and shall deliver him to the gentiles to be mocked and scourged and crucified, and the third day he shall rise again." After the death of Our Lord, the Jews said to Pilate (Matthew xxvii, 63): "We have remembered that that seducer said while he was yet alive: after three days I will rise again." Notice that Christ taught, and was understood by the Jews as teaching, that He would rise from the dead by His own power.

The prophecies use the expressions, "till the Son of man *be risen* (not *raised*)"; *"I will raise* it up"; the third day he shall *rise* (not *be raised*) again"; "after three days *I will rise* again."

Now regarding the great miracle which fulfilled the prophecy, two things must be clearly known: (1) That Christ really died; (2) That Christ really rose again. If these two things are known for certain, then we have certain knowledge that Christ is God; for He is God by the divine approval contained in the wondrous miracle; and He is God by showing Himself master of life and death.

1. *Christ really died.* The four Evangelists testify that Christ died on the Cross. St. Matthew says that He "yielded up the ghost"; and all the others use the expression "gave up the ghost." St. Mark records the report made by the centurion to Pilate, certifying the death of Christ (Mark xv, 45). The soldiers who came to break the legs of the robbers who were crucified with Our Lord, saw that Christ was already dead (John xix, 33), and one of them "opened His side" with a spear, inflicting a wound that was sufficient of itself to cause the death of a man.

When we consider what Our Lord suffered before the Crucifixion: the bloody sweat in the Garden, the still more bloody scourging with metal-tipped thongs, the agonizing and blood-letting crown of thorns pressed hard upon His head, the long exposure through the night and half of another day, during

which His wounds went unattended, the bustle of the
journeys back and forth between the tribunals, the toil
of dragging the heavy Cross to the place of execution—when we consider all this, we must perforce
conclude that Christ would have died before the Crucifixion if some more than human power had not sus-
tained Him so that He might offer the ultimate Sacrifice upon the Tree. And then the Crucifixion itself,
the great wounds that pierced hands and feet and were
kept ever open by the weight of the hanging body,
the agony, the thirst, the pierced side—these of
themselves were more than sufficient to insure His
death. Again, had not some superhuman power kept
Him alive, Christ must certainly have died long before the lapse of the three terrible hours that He suffered upon the Cross.

Christ was buried in the Jewish manner, embalmed
with about one hundred pounds of spices (John xix,
39), bound about with linen cloths (Matthew xxvii,
59; Mark xv, 46; Luke xxiii, 53; John xix, 40), and
shut up in a sepulchre hewn out of the rock. If a man
in perfect health and strength were so bound up,
placed in an almost airless chamber, covered with aro-
matic spices, he would suffocate in an hour. Even if
the death on the Cross were not an established and
indubitable fact, the death of the wounded and worn
out Christ from such a burial, of some forty hours'
duration, would be beyond question.

Certainly, then, Christ died. The brutality of His

treatment during the trial would alone have caused His death in a short time. The Crucifixion alone would have caused it. The pierced side alone would have caused it. The burial alone would have caused it. Surely, no one in his senses can suppose for an instant that Christ, who suffered *all* these things, survived them all.

Christ is admitted on all hands as the greatest, the noblest, the most sublime of human characters. Now, Christ said He would die. Therefore, if He did not die, His prediction was false. But He afterwards approved of its recognition as a prophecy truly fulfilled. Can we suppose, then, that the greatest, noblest, most sublime of all men was only a cheap deceiver? The thought is impossible.

Christ, therefore, really died and was buried.

2. *Christ really rose from the dead.* The Apostles bore testimony to the fact. And the Apostles had nothing to gain by a deception, nor were they the men to try deception upon the raging populace and the mad Pharisees, from whom they had fled in terror when Christ was enduring His Passion. By preaching the risen Christ, the Apostles placed themselves in imminent danger of persecution and death, and they knew it. Still they maintained, even unto death, that Christ had risen by His own power from the dead. The Apostles, then, were certainly not *deceivers* in this matter.

Nor were the Apostles themselves *deceived* about the Resurrection. They were not credulous. At the beginning, they were slow to believe that Christ had really come to life again. In spite of the fact that Our Lord had foretold it to them more than once, His death upon the Cross was so terrible a thing, so shattering a reality, that they were left bewildered. When the women came to tell them of the Resurrection, they were hopeful and eager enough, but they did not take it for a fact until some of them ran to the grave to see for themselves whether the corpse of their beloved Master were not still where it had been laid.

Christ, risen glorious from the tomb, appeared to many. He appeared to Mary Magdalen, to Peter and John, to the two disciples on their way to Emmaus (a village some eight miles from Jerusalem), to the disciples gathered together when Thomas was absent, and again when Thomas was present and was allowed to touch Our Lord and to make certain of the reality of His wounds. And St. Paul testifies (1 Corinthians xv, 6) that on one occasion Christ was seen by more than five hundred at once.

Even the enemies of Christ believed in the Resurrection as a fact, and they did their best to hush the matter up. They offered bribes to the guard that had stood watch at the sepulchre to say that *while they were asleep* the disciples of Jesus stole the body away (Matthew xxviii, 13). Well may St. Augustine say of this frantic and futile gesture: "O unhappy

shrewdness! Do you then trust *sleeping* witnesses?"
How could the soldiers swear to what had taken place
while they slept? This was the ultimate breakdown
of all the plotting of the crafty Pharisees; this was
their last argument against Christ; this was the vain
and half-witted cry of the great "leaders of the people" who had been so sleek and smug and confident in
the outcome of their removal of "that seducer"; this
was the last gasp of their insane fury when they saw
all their schemes defeated; and so blind was their
rage in defeat that they contradicted themselves without noticing their absurdity: "Say you, His disciples
came by night, and stole him away when we were
asleep." The Pharisees knew that the Resurrection
was true, and they hated its truth with a bitterness
past all expressing. They had hated Christ living
among them, they had gloated over Christ dead, and
they feared and hated Christ risen from the grave.
Their very hatred is proof positive that Christ had
really come back to life again; for no man fears his
enemy entombed, and no man hates the shadow and
pretense of one who has been alive, but is now dead.

Christ had plainly said that He would rise from the
dead. If He did not, then He posed as a prophet when
He was not a true prophet. If he did not, then He is a
base and contemptible deceiver. How, then, can men
hold Him admirable, and yet deny His Resurrection?
No, if we admit that Christ is even a good man, we

are forced to admit that His Resurrection is a plain fact. And those that deny the Resurrection are usually the very first to protest that they regard Christ as the greatest of men; that they esteem Him as the noblest and truest of teachers; that they admit Him to be the greatest power and the most lasting influence for good that ever came into the world! They will admit this, but they will contradict themselves by refusing to admit His Resurrection. Truly, the "unhappy shrewdness" of the Pharisees has still a place among men. Those that deny the Resurrection in the name of "freedom of thought" or of that mysterious thing called the "open mind," have neither freedom nor openness, but are closed in the ugly prison of a philosophy that permits neither the one nor the other. A pertinent remark of Mr. G. K. Chesterton comes to mind here, and, even at the risk of slight irrelevance, it shall be inserted (*Orthodoxy*, p. 278 f.) : "Somehow or other an extraordinary idea has arisen that the disbelievers in miracles consider them coldly and fairly, while believers in miracles accept them only in connection with some dogma. The fact is quite the other way. The believers in miracles accept them (rightly or wrongly) because they have evidence for them. The disbelievers in miracles deny them (rightly or wrongly) because they have a doctrine against them."

Christ, therefore, really rose from the dead.

The conclusion which follows upon the fact of Christ's death and Resurrection is inevitable: He is true God who says He is true God and performs such a stupendous miracle in support of His claim. He is God who says He is God and shows Himself God by His mastery over death. Can reason, then, refuse to admit that Jesus Christ is indeed true God?

Certain objections, foolish indeed, but advanced by men of seemingly sound mind, must be answered here. They must be mentioned and answered *because they are themselves proofs of the divinity of Christ.* For these objections show to what lengths of absurdity a man can go in order to argue himself out of belief in a fact that stares him in the face; and, truly, *if it were not a fact,* he would not be so frantically eager to deal with it (even to dispose of it) as to forget the plain requirements of rational thought and begin to gibber.

1. Christ was not dead when He was laid in the tomb; He was worn out, and had passed into a state of trance or coma. Yes, Christ was worn out! Worn and wounded and bruised beyond anything that human nature can survive, He was laid in that airless grave. Wrapped up in linen cloths, covered with a hundredweight of pungent spices, He was sealed in and left for dead. This was on Friday afternoon. Yet on the next Sunday morning—with no intervening care for His wounds, no air, no light, no food—

He rose in full strength, in glorious bodily perfection, and was able to move aside the "very great" stone that closed His grave! On Sunday morning, some forty hours after His burial, the worn-out Christ was able to discard His weakness, to walk firmly upon His pierced feet, aye, and before evening of the same day, He was able to walk eight miles to Emmaus, where He sat at table with two of His disciples! More: merely because He had been in a trance in the tomb, He was now able to appear and disappear at will, to enter through closed doors into the room where His frightened followers were gathered! He was able to stretch out those strained arms without a trace of stiffness or inconvenience; He was able to lift up food with those pierced hands without a sign of discomfort; He was able to endure the hand of Thomas in the wound of His side without a twinge of pain! Surely an "unhappy shrewdness" has suggested this *trance theory* to stubborn minds. And, in addition to its intrinsic absurdity, this theory makes Christ the greatest deceiver that the world has ever known.

2. The disciples of Christ were nervously wrought up by the terrible events of the Passion and Crucifixion; they had been told by Christ that He would rise on the third day; their "expectant attention" made them see visions; they only fancied they saw Christ, for Christ was not really risen, nor was He with them at all.—We have seen that the disciples did

not actually expect the Resurrection. True, Christ
had foretold it, but the prophecy was a terrible thing
for them to take literally; they had certainly thought
that the Lord would somehow fulfil His word without the horrible facts of the Passion and the Cross.
Had not Peter been told that Christ was to be betrayed to the chief priests, and condemned, and
scourged? And did not that same Peter draw his
sword in a furious refusal to believe that such things
had to be? Like many, nay, like all of the pronouncements of Christ, the prophecy of the Resurrection
was not clear in the untrained minds of the Apostles
until the fulness of knowledge came with the descent
of the Holy Ghost. In some dim way they had known
that terrible things were to happen to Christ; yet,
somehow, they felt that their all-powerful Master
would manage the whole matter without actual dis-
aster; and even after the most solemn prophecy and
prayer of Christ, the best beloved of the Apostles
went calmly to sleep. So also, after the Crucifixion
had stunned them with its reality, the disciples hoped
that somehow, in His own mysterious way, the Lord
would rise again, but they certainly did not look for
Him to walk with them, and talk with them, and eat
with them, as He had done before His death. The
news of the Resurrection did not find the Apostles
"expectantly attentive"; they doubted it, and some
of them ran to the tomb to make sure of its truth or
falsity. St. Thomas flatly declared that he did not be-

lieve it; he would accept no testimony; he said that
only the actual presence of Christ would convince
Him of the Resurrection, and, for fear that he should
come to suffer hallucination, he would not even accept
the appearance of Christ as testimony, unless he
could touch Him and make sure of His wounds. The
two disciples on their way to Emmaus did not expect the Resurrection; they said sadly that they had
"hoped that it was he that should have redeemed
Israel," but that hope was obviously only a sorrowful
memory with them. Surely, these two disciples were
not victims of "expectant attention" when they suddenly and unexpectedly recognized Christ in the
breaking of bread. No, the Apostles were not victims
of any hallucination; plain facts render the thought
absurd. Besides, like every theory in denial of the
Resurrection, this theory leaves Christ as the arch-
deceiver of all times! For He had foretold His Resurrection, and if it did not happen as He foretold it,
then He is a false prophet. And yet the doctrine of
this false prophet is the admiration of all men, and
has had power literally to "transform the face of
the earth!"

We conclude, then, that sound human reason cannot escape the recognition of the Resurrection as a
fact, as the fulfilment of a prophecy, and, above all,
as an astounding miracle. We need not pause longer
to examine its *philosophical* truth as a miracle, for
none but God is master of life and death, and if a

man rises from the dead, God is the author of that wonderful resurrection. And since, as we have amply seen, there can be no doubt about the *historical* truth of the miracle, we have no choice but to accept it as absolute evidence of the truth of Christ's doctrine and mission; as proof, absolute and forever incontrovertible, that Christ is very God.

SUMMARY OF THE ARTICLE

In this Article we have reviewed our knowledge of miracles as unquestionable proofs of God's approval of a doctrine or mission as divine. We have verified the miracles of Christ as true miracles, investigating two typical examples to demonstrate their historical and philosophical truth as miracles. Then we have studied the crowning miracle of Christ, the glorious Resurrection from the dead. We have seen that the Resurrection is a most certain fact, and that it is absolute proof that Christ is true God.

ARTICLE 4. JESUS CHRIST PROVED HIMSELF GOD
BY HIS PROPHECIES

a) Prophecies   b) The Prophecies of Christ

a) PROPHECIES

In an earlier Chapter of this manual we have defined prophecies and have shown them to be a certain proof of truth in the doctrine of the prophet. For a prophecy is the certain foreknowledge and pronouncement of a future *free* event, that is, of an event that is not capable of being forecast or conjectured from the mere course of nature, but is, in itself, the result of free choice on the part of a rational being. Now, no knowledge that is circumscribed, no knowledge that falls short of the infinite, can know such future free events; and if a man shows that he has such knowledge, then he either is himself possessed of infinite understanding (and is God) or he speaks as the messenger of the All-Knowing.

b) THE PROPHECIES OF CHRIST

If Christ, therefore, is a true prophet, it follows that He is God or a messenger sent by God, whose message is true. But His message is that He is God. Therefore, in any case, if Christ is a true prophet, He is God.

Now, Christ *is* a true prophet. He made many prophecies of future free events that were so perfectly fulfilled that not even ill-will can assert that His prophecies were mere guesses. No mere conjecture or guess can predict all the details and circumstances of a complex event; and if *many* complete and detailed predictions are literally fulfilled, then the prophet is a true prophet, and reason must acknowledge him as such. Let us consider some of the prophecies of Christ and then look at their fulfilment.

1. Christ foretold all the events of His Passion and

death. In St. Matthew (xx) we read that He told His disciples that, when they had completed a certain journey to Jerusalem, He would be *betrayed, condemned, mocked, scourged,* and *crucified by the Gentiles.* He named His betrayer (Matthew xxvi, 25); He foretold the sum the betrayer would receive for his treachery (John xiii, 21, 26); He foretold the triple denial of St. Peter (xxvi, 34); He prophesied that He would be forsaken by His disciples (Matthew xxvi, 31). These, and other details of His Passion, details that no merely human knowledge could contain, and no mere fortunate conjecture could hit upon, were accurately foretold by Christ. Therefore, He is a true prophet. Therefore, He is God.

2. Christ foretold His Resurrection (John iii, 19; Matthew xvii, 9; xx, 19; xxvii, 63). He declared that He would rise on the third day after His death (Matthew xx, 19), or "three days" after His death, which means the same thing, for the ancient method of computation reckoned each part of a day as "a day." These prophecies were accurately fulfilled. Therefore, Christ is a true prophet. Therefore, Christ is God.

3. Christ foretold His Ascension (John vi, 63), which took place, as we read in Acts i, 9. He foretold the coming of the Holy Ghost (John xiv, 26), which took place (Acts ii, 1–4). These prophecies were accurately fulfilled. Therefore, Christ is a true prophet. Therefore, Christ is God.

4. Christ foretold the rapid growth of His Church,

a thing that depended (humanly speaking) on men's free acceptance of His doctrine. This was, therefore, a prophecy of a future free event. The prophecy (Matthew xiii, 31, 33; xvi, 18) was so quickly fulfilled that, in spite of terrible persecutions, Christianity, within seventy years of the Resurrection, had spread in a fashion that caused the proconsul Pliny to exclaim in amazement and dismay; and by the year 200 Tertullian was able to write, "We [Christians] are but of yesterday, and yet we fill every place that you have, cities, islands, citadels, demesnes." Christ, then, is a true prophet. Therefore, Christ is God.

5. Christ foretold the destruction of Jerusalem (Luke xix, 43, 44) and the dispersion of the Jews (Luke xxi, 23, 24). These prophecies were literally fulfilled. Therefore, Christ is a true prophet. Therefore, Christ is God.

Christ prophesied the endurance of His Church until the end of time (Matthew xxviii, 20) and declared that the gates of hell should not prevail against it (Matthew xvi, 18). These prophecies are in course of fulfilment, and as age after age brings its persecutions against the Church, as age after age passes and leaves the Church still flourishing, we find in these prophecies a greater and truer fulfilment, and we acknowledge with their truth the divinity of Him who pronounced them.

To sum up: A true prophet is a true messenger of

God; his word is necessarily true. But Christ is a true prophet, as we have amply shown. Therefore, His word is true. But His word is that He is God. Therefore, Christ is truly God.

SUMMARY OF THE ARTICLE

In this brief Article we have reviewed our knowledge of prophecies as unquestionable proofs of God's approval of a doctrine or mission as divine. We have verified some of the prophecies of Christ as true prophecies. We have seen that these are unmistakable proofs of the truth of His doctrine. Now, His doctrine proclaims Him to be God. Therefore, we have proved Him to be God.

CHAPTER III

JESUS CHRIST, TRUE MAN

This Chapter gives a brief proof that Jesus Christ, who is true God, is true man also. The Chapter is added for the sake of completeness in showing the Redeemer as the God-Man. No one of any consequence now doubts the true humanity of Christ, but there were heretics in the past who denied it, just as there have been and will be heretics to deny everything and to assert every frantic folly that wild imagination and stubborn bad will can bring forward. Such heretics (like the Docetae and the Apollinarists) asserted that Christ had only the appearance of a man; that His humanity was not genuine, but a sham; that He appeared *in human form,* but not *as a human being.* Now, if Christ is not true man, then Mary is not the Mother of God; then Christ is not truly our Brother; then the Redeemer is not of the race that should atone for sin; then the Redemption loses its character as an atonement *in justice;* then there is no sufficient reason for Christ's coming, and His appearance is in conflict with infinite Wisdom, which does nothing in vain.

The Chapter is not divided into Articles, but presents its brief proof in a direct and simple study.

That Christ is true man is proved simply. Christ said He was man, for He called Himself "the Son of man"; He acknowledged Mary as His Mother; He was truly conceived and born of Mary according to the revealed word; He said He would truly die, which would have been impossible if He were not true man. Now, Christ is God. What He says is divine truth. Therefore, it is divinely true that Christ is man.

If Christ is not true man, then millions are deceived by Him. But He is God, and cannot be a deceiver. Therefore, Christ is true man.

The Scriptures give the list of Christ's human ancestors (Matthew i, 1–17) and show that He is a true descendant of David. He was truly conceived; He was truly born (Luke ii, 7) ; He grew up like other children (Luke ii, 52) ; He acted as a true man, talking, hungering, thirsting, eating, drinking, sleeping, walking, fatigued by travel, shedding blood, scourged, crucified, dead, buried. He was glad, (looking upon the good young man of means who came to Him), troubled, sorrowful even unto death, acting in all as a true man. He exercised acts of religion as man, spending nights in prayer, giving thanks to God the Father, imploring favors and graces for His Apostles. He exercised acts of obedience and humility, proper only in man, and showed human confidence in God by commending His soul into the hands of the Heavenly Father.

Christ, therefore, is true man as well as true God. Now, if He were a complete human *personality* as well as a divine personality, He would be two *persons,* and the person who is really God would not be the same person that is really man : He would not be the God-Man. Therefore, while Christ has the true and full *nature* of man, while He has a true human body and a true human soul with its faculties of understanding and will, He is not a human *person.* He has the nature of man united substantially with the nature of God, and this in the unity of the Second Person of the Blessed Trinity, the Son of God. Christ, therefore, has *two natures* (a divine and a human), but is only *one Person,* and that the second Person of the Blessed Trinity. The union of the two natures is effected in the Person of the Son of God; this substantial union is called the *hypostatic* union, a term which comes from the Greek *hypostasis,* used to signify *a Person* of the Blessed Trinity; hence *the Hypostatic Union* is the union of the two natures (of God and man) in the one Person of the Son of God.

SUMMARY OF THE CHAPTER

This very brief but important Chapter has given us clear argument in proof of the fact that Jesus Christ, who is true God, is also true man. We have added a word (not strictly within the proper scope of Apologetics) on the manner in which the humanity and the divinity are united in Christ.

BOOK FOURTH

THE CHURCH

In Book First we proved that God exists. In Book Second
we proved that the existing God is to be known, loved, and
served, in the practice of the true religion. In Book Third
we proved that Our Lord Jesus Christ is God, and therefore His religion is the true religion. In this Fourth Book
we are to show that the true religion of Christ is that of the
Catholic Church, and no other. The Book is divided into
three Chapters, as follows:

CHAPTER I

THE CHURCH OF JESUS CHRIST

This Chapter shows that Jesus Christ *founded a Church,* and that St. Peter, the Rock of foundation, holds the *primacy,* not only of honor, but also of jurisdiction, in that Church.

The Chapter is divided into two Articles, as follows:
Article 1. The Formation of the Church
Article 2. The Primacy of St. Peter

ARTICLE I. THE FORMATION OF THE CHURCH

a) Meaning of *Church*   b) The Founding of the Church

a) MEANING OF *CHURCH*

The word *church* comes into our language by a roundabout derivation from the Greek *kyriakon,* which means "the Lord's house." Thus *church* literally means a building or place where believers gather to worship God. By extension, the term *church* means the believers themselves, and the word may be defined as: The body of those who believe the same doctrine, observe the same essential worship, and recognize a common religious authority. In other words, a church is *a society* of persons banded together under a common religious authority to achieve their common end (i. e., salvation) by the use of common means.

If Our Lord Jesus Christ founded such a society, He founded *a Church*.

b) THE FOUNDING OF THE CHURCH

Our Lord founded a society such as we have described (i. e., a Church) if He formed a group of His followers into a special body with special ministry, and gave to this body the task of gathering mankind together under their teaching and governing authority for the profession and practice of His true religion. Now, Our Lord did form such a group, and He did give this group such a commission. Therefore, Our Lord founded a Church.

1. *Our Lord formed a special group.* In St. Luke's Gospel (vi, 12–16) we read: "It came to pass in those days that he (i. e., *Christ*) went out into a mountain to pray, and he passed the whole night in the prayer of God. And when day was come, he called unto him his disciples: and *he chose twelve of them whom also he named Apostles:* Simon whom he surnamed Peter, and Andrew his brother, James and John, Philip and Bartholomew, Matthew and Thomas, James the son of Alpheus, and Simon who is called Zelotes, and Jude the brother of James, and Judas Iscariot who was the traitor."

2. *Our Lord gave this group a special ministry.* When a successor to Judas was to be chosen, St. Peter said to the others (Acts i, 15–17): "Brethren, the Scripture must needs be fulfilled . . . concern-

ing Judas . . . who was numbered *with us* and had obtained part *of this ministry.*" Praying God to direct their choice, the disciples said (Acts i, 24, 25): "Thou Lord, who knowest the hearts of all men, shew whether of these two thou hast chosen to take the place of *this ministry and apostleship* from which Judas hath by transgression fallen . . ."

3. *The ministry of the Apostles was to teach and govern all men:* Christ said to the Apostles: "Going therefore, *teach all nations* . . . to *observe all things* whatsoever I have commanded you" (Matthew xxviii, 18–20). Thus the Apostles were to *teach* and *govern* all nations—all mankind. In detail, the Apostles were to baptize (Matthew xxviii, 19), to teach Christ's religion (Matthew xxviii, 20), to offer the sacrifice of the Body and Blood of Christ (John xxii, 19), to loose and bind (Matthew xviii, 18), to forgive sins (John xx, 23), to exercise Christ's own authority (John xx, 21).

Christ, therefore, founded a Church. In founding the central teaching and governing body as the core and nucleus of the whole Church, Christ established *the teaching Church* and gave it commission to enlist the *believing* or the *learning* Church. The teaching and the learning Church together make up the one undivided Church of Jesus Christ.

This Church was founded for all men of all times. Christ said, "Teach *all nations*, . . . and behold I am with you *all days* even to the consummation of the world." (Matthew xxviii, 18–20).

In commissioning His Apostles, Christ established His Church. And in establishing His Church, He arranged for the spread of His religion. He did not command His teaching Church, His commissioned Apostles, to prepare documents or scriptures; He commanded them to go and teach, and baptize, and forgive sins, and offer Mass (John xxii, 19), and require obedience from men to "all things whatsoever I have commanded," i. e., to the whole of His religion. Christ Himself has left no written line or word of instruction, nor did He ever tell His Apostles to write. The Holy Scripture is indeed the word of God, yet we see from the founding of the Church that it is not the sole means, nor the most important means, for the enlightenment and salvation of mankind.

Christ is God, and His Church is the Church of God. Therefore, all men are required to know it, to recognize it, to belong to it, to live up to its requirements. Those who realize this obligation, or who might easily recognize it by giving even a little serious thought to this all-important matter, cannot hope for salvation if they remain out of Christ's Church.

SUMMARY OF THE ARTICLE

We have seen in this brief but very important article that Christ, in commissioning His Apostles to teach and govern mankind in His name and by His authority, founded *a Church*. We have seen that the Church is the means for the enlightenment and salvation of the world. We have paused upon the point of man's obligation to know and to belong to the true Church of Christ. In a later Chapter we shall show that the true Church of Christ is the Catholic Church and no other.

ARTICLE 2. THE PRIMACY OF ST. PETER

a) Meaning of *Primacy*   b) St. Peter's Office

a) MEANING OF *PRIMACY*

The word *primacy* is derived from the Latin *primus,* "first," It is the state or office of being the *first* or *chief* officer in a society. The primacy of St. Peter means the office which St. Peter held (and which his successor holds to-day), that is, the *first place* in the Church of Christ. And it is not merely the first place in honor or dignity, but the first place in jurisdiction, in authority. When we say that Christ conferred the primacy on St. Peter (and his successors), we mean that He made St. Peter His vicar, His vicegerent, His direct representative clothed with his own authority, infallibly guided to lead men aright by exercising the office of universal teacher of faith and morals.

b) ST. PETER'S OFFICE

To prove that St. Peter (and his successors, each in turn) received such a *primacy* as we have defined above, it will be necessary to establish the following facts: (1) That Christ singled out St. Peter for a peculiar office, distinct from that of the other Apostles, of teaching and governing *the whole Church* by his *supreme* authority; (2) That Christ actually conferred upon St. Peter the duties and powers of that office; (3) That St. Peter actually exercised that office.

1. *Christ singled out St. Peter for the Primacy.* Christ is, and ever must remain, the Head of His Church. Yet Christ made the Church a visible society, the service and value of which must be realized here in this visible world. The Church then had to have a *visible* head. Christ, however, was to ascend into Heaven, and to be no longer visible as Man upon earth. It is the very nature and logic of this situation that requires a visible head of the Church *on earth.* Now, Christ singled out St. Peter as this head, for:

(a) Christ made Peter the Rock upon which the Church is builded. After Peter had professed the divinity of Christ, Our Lord said to him (Matthew xvi, 18) : "I say to *thee:* That *thou art* Peter (i. e., *Rock*) and upon this rock I will build my church, and the gates of hell shall not prevail against it." Notice the singular pronoun. This declaration had reference to Peter *alone,* and not to the other Apostles. Again: Christ made a special prayer for Peter, that he might not fail, telling him that the devil had wished to conquer him particularly (in view of his supreme office), and ordering Peter to *confirm* the others (Luke xxii, 31, 32) : "Simon, Simon, behold Satan hath desired to have you that he may sift you as wheat : but I have prayed for *thee* that *thy* faith fail not : and *thou* being once converted, confirm *thy* brethren." Notice again that the singular pronoun makes the declaration refer to Peter alone. Peter was to *confirm*, i. e., to *strengthen* the Church as a true and solidly built foundation.

(b) Christ conferred on Peter alone the "keys," i. e., the supreme mastership of the Kingdom of Heaven, the Church. He said to Peter (Matthew xvi, 19) : "I will give to *thee* the keys of the kingdom of heaven. And whatsoever *thou* shalt bind upon earth, it shall be bound also in heaven : and whatsoever *thou* shalt loose upon earth, it shall be loosed also in heaven."

2. *Christ actually conferred the Primacy upon St. Peter.* The promises of Christ, who is the all-perfect God as well as Man, are sufficient to account for the conferring of the promised office ; for God necessarily fulfils His promises. Still, we have a special and separate ceremony in which the office was actually conferred. After the Resurrection, on the occasion of His third appearance before His disciples, Christ singled out Peter and said to him (John xxi, 15–17) : "Simon, son of John, lovest thou me more than these? He saith to him : Yea Lord, thou knowest that I love thee. He saith to him : *Feed my lambs.* He saith

to him again: Simon, son of John, lovest thou me? He saith to him: Yea Lord, thou knowest that I love thee. He saith to him; *Feed my lambs.* He saith to him the third time: Simon, son of John, lovest thou me? Peter was grieved, because he had said to him the third time, Lovest thou me? And he said to him: Lord, thou knowest all things: thou knowest that I love thee. He said to him: *Feed my sheep."* Thus the whole flock of Christ, sheep and lambs, was placed under the supreme shepherdship of St. Peter. The solemnity of the occasion, the repetition of the question, the impressive insistence of Our Lord upon an answer, His no less impressive commission when the answer was given—all these circumstances mark this act of Our Lord as no ordinary act, but as one of deep significance. Christ had often spoken of His Church as a sheepfold, and in the solemn words of this text He made Peter (and, as we shall see, his successors, each in turn) the supreme shepherd, the supreme authority, in the Church.

3. *Peter actually exercised the Primacy.* Peter, though not the oldest Apostle, nor the first called by Christ, took charge of the Church immediately after the Ascension of Christ. He presided at the election of Matthias to the place left vacant by the defection of Judas. He was the spokesman for all the Apostles when the people, amazed at the "power of tongues," knew not what to think or say of them. He definitely settled the question of admitting the Gentiles to the

Church. He presided at the meeting or "council" of the Apostles at Jerusalem. (For all these matters, see Acts, i, ii, xi, xv.) The exercise of the primacy by Peter was always recognized as right and proper. The Evangelists always mention Peter first in any list, complete or partial, of the Apostles, and St. Matthew says (x, 2) : "The names of the twelve apostles are these : The *first:* Simon who is called Peter . . ." The tradition of the Church (with many quotable citations available from the Fifth century onwards) has ever recognized the exercise of the primacy as a historical fact in Peter's case, and as the right and duty of his successor. Indeed, in the Council of Ephesus (Third General or Œcumenical Council of the Church) it was plainly stated that every age had recgonized St. Peter, prince of the Apostles, as the foundation and chief authority in the Church, and the Pope then reigning (Celestine) stood to St. Peter as "his successor in order and the holder of his place."

Since Peter's office did not die with Peter, and since the Church and her mission is for "all nations . . . all days," the office of St. Peter must obviously descend to his legitimate successor. Even as the Apostles were not to be deprived of the fulness of "this ministry and apostleship" by the treason and death of Judas, but elected a successor to be with them the "witness of Christ's resurrection," so the Church is not to be left without the necessary ministry and apostleship of its visible head. Christ promised to re-

main with the Church "even to the consummation of
the world." That the Church must exist "all days,"
is, therefore, a certainty; and, if it is to exist as Christ
formed it, it must have its visible head. And this
head must be—as the Church has ever logically believed and taught—the successor of St. Peter, clothed
with St. Peter's power and authority. The successor
of St. Peter is the Pope, the Bishop of Rome, Supreme Pontiff of the Church.

The supreme head of the Church, he whose office is
that of feeding the flock of Christ, must, in the essential matters of faith and morals, be actually unable to poison that flock with erroneous teaching. In
a word, Peter (and his successors, each in turn) must
be *infallible* when, as teacher and ruler of the whole
Church, he speaks in definite pronouncement upon a
matter of *faith* (what is to be believed as of Apostolic
revelation) or *morals* (what is right or wrong, good
or bad, in human conduct). This claim to infallibility
is sometimes regarded by those outside the Catholic
Church as monstrous—and so it would be if it were
a mere human claim or pretense. But it is not only
reasonable, but actually *requisite,* when we consider
what the Supreme Pontiff has to do. Can he—teaching the whole Church in an essential matter of faith
or morals in the name of Christ and by His authority—teach falsehood? Christ, then, is falsified!
Can he—commissioned as he is to feed the flock
of Christ—feed it the poison of error? As a man the

Pope may be weak, sinful, fallible; but when he speaks *officially* to the *whole Church* in a matter of *faith or morals,* then he is exercising the office Christ gave him to exercise; then he is speaking in the very power and authority of Christ; then he is the spokesman of Christ Himself—and shall Christ's spokesman be able to teach falsehood to Christ's faithful? If so, then *Christ Himself is deceived and His word falsified,* for, if error could be definitely taught and universally accepted as truth in His Church, the gates of hell *could and would* prevail against the Church.

SUMMARY OF THE ARTICLE

In this Article we have defined *primacy* and have seen that the primacy of Christ's Church was actually conferred on St. Peter by Our Lord Himself. We have seen that this primacy descends to the successors of St. Peter in the office of supreme authority in the Church. We have seen that the primacy involves, of necessity, the prerogative of *infallibility,* so that the holder of the primacy (St. Peter, and the Popes, his successors, each in turn) cannot teach falsehood, cannot err, when, as teacher of the universal Church, he speaks authoritatively in a matter of faith or morals.

CHAPTER II

THE MARKS AND ATTRIBUTES OF THE CHURCH OF JESUS CHRIST

In the last Chapter we saw that Christ founded a Church. In the present Chapter we discuss the *character* of that Church. Since the Church is an institution founded for all men by the all-wise God-Man, it must have *marks* by which men may recognize it, and, at the same time, recognize their duty of entering it and living up to its requirements. Further, the Church being what it is—an institution divinely founded—it must possess certain properties or *attributes* that characterize it alone. To find the true *character* of the Church of Christ, we must look for its *characteristics;* and its *characteristics* are *marks* and *attributes.*

The present Chapter is divided into two Articles:

 Article 1. The Marks of the Church
 Article 2. The Attributes of the Church

ARTICLE 1. THE MARKS OF THE CHURCH

a) Meaning and Value of *Marks* b) The Marks in Detail

a) MEANING AND VALUE OF MARKS

Our Lord, as we have seen, founded a Church. Since Our Lord is God, His is the true Church to which all men are bound to belong. He has given command that all belong to it in the commission given to the Apostles (the Teaching Church) to teach, bap-

248

tize, and govern "all nations . . . all days, even to the consummation of the world."

Now, Our Lord is Infinite Wisdom. Therefore, He does not found a Church, and require all men to belong to it, without *marking* it unmistakably for their recognition. Indeed, He has Himself compared His Church (the Kingdom of God on earth) to a "city set on a hill, that cannot be hid." The Church of Jesus Christ has, therefore, unmistakable *marks* by which it can be known.

Now, a *mark* is an indication, a sign, a token. It is something that points a thing out, indicates it. In looking for the marks of the Church, we look for such "pointers" and "indicators," such signs and tokens, as are inseparable from it and show it to be what it is. The value of such marks is apparent from the consideration of their necessity, already mentioned in the opening paragraphs of this section.

b) THE MARKS IN DETAIL

Let us begin our study here by assuming the role of a man who is looking for the true Church of Christ. The man says : "I know that Christ founded a Church to which I am bound to belong. I wish to find that Church. Let me consider how I shall know it when I come upon it.

"First, I shall expect the Church, the *true* Church of Christ, to be without *self-contradiction*. Wherever I find its recognized members and teachers, I shall

find the same doctrine taught, the same truths believed. I shall expect variations of ceremonial, I shall
expect differences of language in ritual, I shall expect
differences of disciplinary law for different peoples
and times. But I shall certainly not expect to find
different faiths or different essential worship. In
these, the true Church must be *one*. For, surely, if I
find differences in these things (faith and worship),
I shall find a plurality of religions, not *one* religion,
and certainly Christ taught only one religion. I shall
not listen to people who tell me that I may be vaguely
satisfied with cultivating the "spirit of Christ" and,
for the rest, believing what I like. How can I have
the spirit of Christ unless I have an ardent interest
in knowing what He taught? How can I have the
spirit of Christ if I believe what I like? I want to
believe what is *true,* whether I like it or not: I want
to believe *the very truth* that Christ taught. What
could be the point or purpose of Christ in founding a
Church if people were merely to cultivate a vague and
misty self-satisfaction? People could do *that* without
a Church, without Apostles being appointed and sent
to death in manifestation of truth, without a clear-
cut faith for which thousands have been ready to die.
Nor shall I listen to those that tell me that essential
differences in the many religions that claim to be of
Christ are *not* essential differences. Why, here is one
who says infant baptism is not necessary; here is an-

other who says it *is* necessary for salvation. Shall I
dare to think that these two persons differ in non-
essentials, when the very issue of their disagreement
is the matter of the eternal salvation of immortal
souls? Here is a man who says that the Eucharist or
Lord's Supper is only a highly symbolic and solemn
ceremony, but that the bread and wine are bread and
wine throughout the ceremony, and nothing more;
here is another who declares that the bread and wine
become the actual Body and Blood, Soul and Divinity,
of Jesus Christ. Shall I be imbecile enough to think
this difference non-essential, when it involves the very
question of adoration or idolatry, of due worship or
horrible profanation? No, I must not benumb my
mind into accepting *contradictions* as non-essential
differences, and attributing these to the teaching of
the all-wise Christ. I must find a Church that is uni-
formly *one and the same* in doctrine and worship,
else I shall not have found the Church of Christ. For
Christ taught one doctrine, He founded one Church,
He gave one commission to the Apostles, and that not
a vague or indefinite, but a clear and practical thing.
The *authority* of Christ is also one, and He communicated that single authority to the Church, and in
the Church to St. Peter and his successors. I shall,
therefore, know that I have not found Christ's Church
until I shall have found a Church that is one and the
same in doctrine, in worship, and in authority. Surely,

reason teaches me this at the outset. The first *mark*, therefore, of the Church of Christ is *unity:* it must be *one.*

"Suppose, then, that I shall presently come upon a Church that seems to meet my requirements—and, after all, they are not mine; they are the requirements of common sense and sound reason—shall I be content with unity alone? No, I shall look for something else. Christ founded His Church to lead men safely to God. Now, a man who is safely on the way to God, i. e., to salvation, is a man of virtue and of piety: in a word, he is sanctified, he is *holy.* I read in Scripture (I Thessalonians iv, 3) that God wills man's sanctification, man's holiness; and surely Christ's Church is to help man to do God's will and be saved. The Church of Christ was founded to teach and govern all men, and surely *sanctification, making men holy,* must be the end and purpose of that teaching and government. Therefore, the Church of Christ must teach a holy doctrine; it must govern men with a view to their growth in virtue; in a word, it must show itself *holy.* And it must show some success in its work of sanctifying men; it must really make holy those that are its representative members, those that truly live up to its teachings, not only in letter, but also in spirit. Of course, I know that there will be, that there are, members of the true Church who are not holy. There was an unholy member in the Apostolic Church. And Christ, by His parables of the wheat and cockle, of the net of good fishes and bad, of the unworthy wedding-guest, has plainly taught me what my common sense ought to make clear to me in any case. I know many men who belong to societies; some of them are interested and active members who really represent their organizations; others are slackers who will never attend a meeting nor pay their dues unless pressure is brought to bear upon them, and sometimes not then. Shall I judge a society by its unworthy members? I know many splendid physicians, and I know a few quacks. Shall I judge the medical profession, by reason of the quacks, as a group of unscrupulous and ignorant men who prey upon their fellows and trifle with human health and life? I know many good and learned men of law, and I know, unfortunately, some lawyers of the 'shyster' variety. Because of this latter knowledge, shall I judge the whole legal profession dishonest? Obviously not; I shall not be such a fool as to judge *any* group, *any* society, *any* profession by its *non-representative* members. Nor shall I take mere external conduct as the test of the representative character of any member: for the unworthy clubman wears his lapel-button; the quack looks more learned than any doctor can possibly be; the shyster talks most sagely of the law. No, I shall be fair and honest in this matter. I shall look for the holiness of the Church of Jesus Christ to show in the lives and conduct of those members who are truly and spiritually devoted

to the faith for which that Church stands. It may be
difficult for me to discern this inner loyalty and spirit
in my living fellowmen; but history ought to be full
of illumination on the point. On this score, then, I
shall look for the Church to be holy because its
Founder is Holiness itself, because its doctrine is His
most holy doctrine, and because the purpose of the
true Church must be to make men holy. The second
mark of the Church, therefore, is *holiness*.

"Well, suppose I find a Church which appears to be
both *one* and *holy*. Have I any further test to apply
to it, lest I be deceived by mere *apparent* unity and
holiness? Yes, I look for something else. Christ
founded His Church for all nations . . . all days. I
realize, of course, that the whole world was not
brought into His Church at once, and by that very
word of His. No, the work of conversion was *gradual,* although miraculously swift in the beginning.
The institution of the Church was obviously the plac-
ing of the Church in the world for all men to recognize and enter. I shall look for a Church, then, that is,
in fact, very widespread in its membership; and I
shall look for a church that is without bar or hindrance to any nation, caste, class, or group of men.
In a word, I shall look for the Church that is *universal,* or, as the Greek derivative expresses it, *catholic.* I understand quite well that many men may never
know of Christ or of His Church; I hold that these
are provided for in God's own way, and that they are

really members of the *soul* of the true Church if they use their natural power of reasoning to recognize their duty to God, and use their will to accomplish that duty. I do not look for God to work miracles to accomplish what men can accomplish by missionary activity, nor do I expect God to upset, by miraculous means, what man has done from the first sin onwards to the present day. But I do expect the Church of Christ to be a 'world figure'; I do expect it to be very far-reaching in its existence and its influence; I do expect it to exist, or at least to be known, in every country of the earth. In a word, I expect the Church to be *universal*. And I have a right to expect this of a Church founded for 'all nations,' a Church whose first priests and bishops were sent 'into the whole world' to teach, govern, and sanctify all men. The actual number of members, however, or the number of national groups found in the Church, will not affect its universality. It is sufficient (since men remain free to reject even the Church of God) if the Church *exists,* or at least *is known,* in all lands (at the present stage of advancement in discovery and exploration of the earth), and that no nation or group is excluded from membership in it. The third *mark,* therefore, of the Church of Christ is *universality* or *catholicity.*

"It will not satisfy me to find a Church that is one, holy, and catholic, unless I also find it with an unbroken history, an uninterrupted existence in the world from the time that it was founded. The Church of Christ was founded for 'all days, even to the consummation of the world.' Against this Church the powers or 'gates' of hell were never to prevail, never to cause its extinction even for a short time. Christ is God, and He said His Church would endure 'all days'; He said the gates of hell should not prevail against it; and His word is God's word; His word is the truth. Therefore, in looking for the Church of Christ, I look for a Church that is traceable back to the Apostles, upon whom it was founded. I look for the Church that teaches what the Apostles taught, that is governed by the lineal and lawful successors of the Apostles, and, in special, is presided over by the successor of St. Peter in the primacy. In a word, I look for an *Apostolic* Church. The fourth *mark,* therefore, of the Church of Christ is *Apostolicity.*

"If I find in the world a Church that is truly *One, Holy, Catholic* or *Universal,* and *Apostolic,* I shall know, without doubt of possibility of doubt, that I have found the true Church of Christ. Reason teaches me to look for these marks in the true Church; reason requires no further marks, and will be satisfied with no less."

SUMMARY OF THE ARTICLE

In this Article we have followed a quest of *reason,* and have seen that the reasonable man in search of

Christ's Church must look for that Church which is characterized by *four marks,* viz., Unity, Holiness, Catholicity, Apostolicity. These, then, are the Four Marks of The True Church. In the next Chapter we shall make direct inquiry as to which of the existing Churches actually has these four marks.

ARTICLE 2. THE ATTRIBUTES OF THE CHURCH

a) Meaning of *Attribute*   b) The Attributes in Detail

a) MEANING OF *ATTRIBUTE*

We have already learned the meaning of *attribute* in our study of the Nature and Attributes of God (Book I, Chap. II, Art. 2, a). Here we briefly recall the matter. An *attribute* is a perfection that belongs to the very nature of a thing, and belongs to it by reason of its nature (i. e., because the thing is what it is), but is not a *part* or *element* of the thing. Reasoning is an attribute of man. When a man is fully a man—not an infant, not hampered by defect, imbecility, unconsciousness, or other cause—he will reason inevitably. The actual exercise of the reasoning faculty is not a part or element of man; and yet man will inevitably perform that exercise when his nature is integrally constituted and unthwarted. Reasoning is, therefore, an attribute of man. An attribute is also a *property,* i. e., it is found in the thing of which it is an attribute and *in that thing alone.* Thus reasoning is found in man alone. Reasoning means working a thing out mentally by progressive and logical steps. God knows all things perfectly and eternally; He has no need to study or think things out. Angels know by direct intuition, and do not need to study or "reason" things out. Only man, of intelligent creatures, can reason or has need to reason. Hence, reasoning is *proper* to man alone, and it *marks and characterizes* man. Thus we see that a knowledge of attributes of a thing is a knowledge of marks and characteristics of that thing. In studying the attributes of a thing, we learn what the nature of the thing is. And, conversely, if we know what a thing is, we can reason out what its attributes must be.

Now we know what the Church is. It is an institution of God (for Christ is God) for the salvation of men. All men are called to it. All are to subject themselves by true faith to what it teaches (for it is of God, and teaches truth), by submission to what it rules in matters of morality (for it is of God, and rules rightly), and by obedience to its requirements in the way of worship (for it is of God, and has authority).

We know what the Church is. Let us reason, then, in the person of one who knows that he is a member of the true Church, to discover what its attributes must be. Then, in the person of a sincere seeker for the true Church, we can use the same attributes as unmistakable signs and characteristics pointing to the thing for which we seek.

b) THE ATTRIBUTES IN DETAIL

The true Church is a *visible* society—else it could not serve men. It stands out before men's eyes like "a city set on a hill." It is a world-figure. It consists of men who teach and men who are taught, of men who openly profess its faith, of men who meet visibly in its public worship. And Christ required it to be so, for He sent the Apostles to teach (and hence required the hearers to learn); He sent the Apostles to baptize, and Baptism is conferred by an open and visible rite; He sent the Apostles to govern men in the observance of "all things whatsoever I have commanded you," and that observance must have its outer expression as well as its inner acceptance; He sent His Apostles to men to give them to understand that "everyone that shall confess me *before men,* I will also confess him before my Father who is in heaven. . . . He that shall deny me *before men,* I will also deny him before my Father who is in heaven" (Matthew x, 32). The Church, then, is a visible society. And it has four marks: it is One, it is Holy, it is Catholic (or Universal), and it is Apostolic.

Such being the Church, the believing member of it reasons as follows: "The Church teaches me; it requires that I believe its teachings. It points out Christ's words to me, and I read what He said in founding His Church and sending out the Apostles (Mark xvi, 16): 'Go . . . preach the gospel. . . . He that believeth not shall be condemned.' On pain of damnation, therefore, I am to believe what the Apostolic Church teaches. Surely, then, this Church *cannot* teach me what is false in doctrine or wrong in morality. The gates of hell are not to prevail against the Church; I have Christ's word for it (Matthew xvi, 18), and Christ is the all-knowing and all-truthful God. Then the Church must be literally *unable* to err in doctrine or morality; for if it *could* err, the gates of hell *could* prevail against it, and, without question, *would* prevail. Again: when some special doctrine is subjected to discussion, when human minds cannot agree as to whether it is revealed of God or no, the Church must decide—who else is there? And surely the Church *cannot* decide wrongly. If it could, there is no knowing at all whether a doctrine be of God. In a word, if the Church could err, then I am bound under pain of damnation to belong to a Church that may, through error, teach me falsehood and guide me to sin; a Church that may be prevailed against by the powers of hell; and a Church that is powerless to represent God and declare what is His doctrine. And yet, I have Christ's word that this same Church speaks in His name, is to be heard as Himself, is to guide me to sanctification and salvation. Surely, then, reason tells me that the Church *cannot* err in doctrine or morals. To say that it can err is to say that it is at once Christ's Church, the agency of salvation, and *not* Christ's Church, but a potential agency of damnation! I conclude perforce, by cold reason, that the Church of Christ cannot err in doctrine or morality. In a word, I conclude that the Church, being what it is, has the *attribute* of *infallibility.*

"I have reasoned that I must obey the Church because it is founded by Christ who is God, and who commands me to obey it and believe its teachings. Thus, I perceive at once that the Church has the right and duty of teaching and governing its members, and of exacting acceptance and obedience. In a word, the Church, being what it is, has the *attribute* of *authority.*

"The Church is founded by Christ (who is God) to teach all men 'all days, even to the consummation of the world.' Therefore, the Church, as Christ founded it, must last to the end of time. It cannot fail or disappear from the world. It may be persecuted; its members may be reduced in numbers; but it cannot die out and disappear. If it could, surely the gates of hell would prevail against it; surely Christ would not then 'be with it all days.' As it is, it must remain— one, holy, catholic, Apostolic, infallible, exercising God's communicated authority. The Church, then, being what it is, has the *attribute* of *indefectibility.*"

The seeker for the true Church says, "I recognize the justice of your reasoning. Therefore, in my search for the true Church, I shall have ever before my mind's clear vision the character of the thing I am looking for. I shall look for that Church which is one, holy, catholic, and Apostolic. I shall require this Church to show evidence in its history of *authoritative* rule and pronouncement in matters of faith and morals, and I shall find in its Apostolic continuance sufficient proof of its indefectibility. I shall know this Church as the true and infallible teacher and ruler of men's souls. I shall know it, in a word, as the true Church of Christ.

"Now, where shall I find such a Church? It must be here in this world, for Christ founded it here, and it exists indefectibly. Where is it? I have its marks and attributes clearly in mind; I have my tests ready. Where is the Church that can meet these tests?"

In the next Chapter we shall answer the question of the seeker for the true Church.

SUMMARY OF THE ARTICLE

In this Article we have reasoned out the *attributes* or *properties* of the Church as Infallibility, Authority, and Indefectibility. We led up to the question of attributes by a consideration of the fact that the Church is, of necessity, *a visible society*. We might even align this last point with the attributes, naming four, viz., Visibility, Infallibility, Authority, and Indefectibility.

CHAPTER III

THE IDENTIFICATION OF THE CHURCH OF JESUS CHRIST

In Chapter First we proved that Christ founded a Church. In Chapter Second we discovered what the marks and attributes of that Church must be. In the present Chapter we show that these unmistakable marks and attributes are found in the Holy Roman Catholic Church alone. In other words, we identify the Church of Jesus Christ as the Roman Catholic Church.

The Chapter identifies the Church on the score of marks and attributes, and then briefly indicates the obvious necessity of belonging to the Catholic Church. This matter is discussed in two Articles:

Article 1. The Catholic Church the Church of Christ
Article 2. The Necessity of the Catholic Church

Article 1. The Catholic Church the Church of Christ

a) Meaning of *the Catholic Church*   b) Marks of the Catholic Church   c) Attributes of the Catholic Church

a) MEANING OF *THE CATHOLIC CHURCH*

By *the Catholic Church* (sometimes called the *Roman* Catholic Church because its visible head, the successor of St. Peter, the Pope, is Bishop of Rome) we mean the congregation of all those who profess

263

the faith of Christ, partake of the same Sacraments, and are governed by their lawful pastors under one visible head.

Those who deny any of the doctrines of the faith of Christ, which is found in its integrity in the Catholic Church alone, are, if unbaptized, called *infidels* or *unbelievers;* if baptized (thus claiming to be *Christians*), they are called *heretics.* Those who are baptized and claim to be Christians and accept the faith of Christ, but refuse to acknowledge the unique governing power vested in the visible head of the Church, are called *schismatics.* Since the truth of St. Peter's appointment to the primacy is a truth of the faith itself, *schismatics* are also *heretics.*

Those that claim to be Christians may be divided into three groups, viz., members of the so-called Orthodox Greek Church, Protestants, Catholics. By the Catholic Church we mean the congregation of all those who are properly called Christians, and who are members of neither the Orthodox Greek Church, nor of any Protestant sect, but of the Roman Catholic Church alone.

b) MARKS OF THE CATHOLIC CHURCH

We have seen that the true Church of Jesus Christ must be characterized by the marks of Unity, Holiness, Universality or Catholicity, and Apostolicity. The Catholic Church alone makes any real claim to the possession of these characteristics. Therefore, the

Catholic Church alone makes any real claim to be the true Church of Jesus Christ. Let us see whether her claim is justified:

1. *The Catholic Church is truly one.* Catholics the world over profess one and the same faith; they partake of the same Sacraments, acknowledging *seven* Sacraments, neither more nor less; they have the one Sacrifice of the Body and Blood of Christ in the Mass; they all recognize the one common authority of the successor of St. Peter, the Roman Pontiff. Thus the Catholic Church, the world over, is one in faith or doctrine, one in essential worship, one in government and authority. Obviously, the Catholic Church makes no false claim to unity, but is really *one.*

No other Christian group than the Catholic Church is one. Such groups are not one in government or authority, for they have no common head or rule. They are not one in doctrine, for the Orthodox Greeks deny the doctrine of the primacy as vested in St. Peter and his successors in office, and they are split into different "independent" groups; and Protestants claim the right to interpret Holy Scripture at will, each believing what he chooses by *private judgment.*

2. *The Catholic Church is truly holy.* No one who recites the Apostles' Creed, which is a summary of Catholic belief, can doubt the holiness of her doctrine. She preaches "Christ and Him crucified" to her children, teaching them to restrain passion, to cultivate and practise virtue, to carry the cardinal virtues of

prudence, justice, fortitude, and temperance, to a stage of development far beyond what unaided nature can hope to achieve. She sanctifies the essential human relations of husband and wife, parent and child, ruler and subject. She inculcates a morality that knows no subterfuge, no tricky adaptation to convenience, no change. She stands squarely against the evils that come from the weak human quest of comfort and softness, and requires her children to bear the Cross of Christ in fidelity to the end, keeping their minds upon the truth that "we have not here a lasting city," and filling their hearts with hope of that which we look for and which is to come to those that persevere in justice unto the end. She raises men's minds to high ideals; she can point to a myriad of institutions for the care of the sick and poor, for the education of the young, for the rescue of the erring— institutions of men and women who have freely sacrificed worldly honor and comfort, and have bound themselves by a solemn vow to the marvellous perfections of poverty, chastity, and obedience in all things lawful to their spiritual superiors. Her Sacraments, instituted by Christ, bring grace, peace, courage, hope, and joy beyond man's fondest dreams. The Church makes men holy, and has made millions holy. No one with a knowledge of history can doubt the holiness of Francis of Assisi, of Teresa, of Benedict, of Charles Borromeo, and thousands of other men and women who are great historical personages; nor can one doubt what *made* these persons holy—it was their religion, its truth, its Sacraments. Other bodies of Christians may claim a few martyrs; the Catholic Church points to her thousands and tens of thousands of martyrs. Martyrdom alone is not a proof of truth, for men may die for a mistake, they may even die for what they know to be untrue. But thousands and thousands of men and women and children do not die for one and the same thing, thousands of others do not endure persecution and evils worse than death for that same thing, unless the thing be true and worthy. Other bodies of Christians have outstanding heroes of virtue; the Church points to her hundreds of thousands of *saints*—men, women, and children, whose lives are nearly all available to us in the records of human history. Great heroism is not in itself a proof of truth, for men may be heroic for mistaken ideals; but hundreds of thousands of all ages, of both sexes, of all periods of history, are not heroic for the same mistake.

No non-Catholic Christian body can justify a claim to holiness. Many persons may lead individual lives of great perfection as members of a non-Catholic religious group; but the group itself cannot claim holiness. For the founders of such groups were not holy. It would appear invidious to mention here the private characters of men like Luther and Henry VIII. Nor were the mistaken zealots who founded certain sects holy men; they lacked moderation, justice, and humility. Besides, the holiest *man* cannot presume of his own authority to set up a religion to make other men holy; the very presumption is a proof of his own lack of holiness. Only God can found a Church; only God can truly establish means for the sanctification and salvation of men; only God can communicate such means to His church for the welfare of her members and of all the world. Christ is God; Christ's Church is God's Church; and no existing body of Christians other than the Catholic Church can even reasonably *claim* to be instituted by Christ Himself.

3. *The Catholic Church is truly universal or catholic.* From the time of Christ the Church has existed, and she has spread to every part of the world. She still continues to grow and to fulfil the command of her Founder (Mark xvi, 15) : "Go ye into the whole world, and preach the gospel to every creature." Other religious bodies exist in this age or that; they exist in this country or that; but the Catholic Church alone can claim existence in every age since Christ and among all peoples.

No non-Catholic Christian group can justify a claim to universality. Such groups are all of recent origin; ages upon ages passed in which they were unknown. They have not spread through all the world, nor are they spreading. They have split up into innumerable sects and sub-sects until, at the present time, the little life that they took with them in their separation from Catholicism has mostly disappeared.

The Greek Orthodox Church seems to have gone to shreds since the World War, and it takes no unkindly observer to notice that Protestantism as a religion is dead. For years now, the average Protestant pulpit has been content with the drooling of platitudes and with intermittent attacks "on Rome." Indeed, many outstanding clergymen of different Protestant groups preach openly that Jesus Christ is not God! Nor have Protestant sects, or Protestantism if you prefer the term, kept the morality of Christ's Church intact. As these lines are written, a brisk rebellion of *clergymen* against their bishop is going forward in New York City. And the cause of the uproar is this: a Protestant bishop had the sanity and the Christian courage to denounce a man of wide influence for teaching the propriety of the impure thing called "companionate marriage": the clergymen do not think their bishop is justified in taking such an "extreme" view of moral requirements as to insist upon the observance of the Sixth Commandment and upon the respect that is due to the sanctity of Christian marriage!—Protestantism is not universal. Indeed, we should find it hard to define the term *Protestantism* and to declare what, in way of religion, it really stands for. Even if we use the name as a blanket-term for all the different sects, and call that *the Church* (which is strictly in the modern manner), we shall at once perceive the absurdity of attributing anything like universality to *that* woeful welter of

conflicting theories (if they are definite enough to
be called theories), to *that* chaos of muddled sentiments and abortive half-thoughts.

4. *The Catholic Church is truly Apostolic.* Human
history brings the proofs; the history of the Catholic
Church goes back unbroken to the Apostles. The doctrine of the Church is the doctrine committed by
Christ to the Apostles, preached by the Apostles, and
contained in Holy Scripture and Apostolic Tradition.
No *new* "dogmas" or solemn pronouncements of
articles of belief have since been made by the Church.
When the Church, the infallible teacher of Christ's
truth, has been called upon for a pronouncement, a
"dogma" of faith, this has always been the clearing
up of a point of Apostolic doctrine about the character of which confusion existed in the minds of the
learned. Thus, the Immaculate Conception of the
Mother of God was not defined as a "dogma" until
1854. But it was not a *new* article of faith. Every
Catholic had always received and believed it. Every
age had admitted it. Reason itself suggests, nay, demands it. But the question settled by the pronouncement of 1854 was this: Is this doctrine, which we all
believe, which all Catholics have always believed,
really a part of the divine faith committed to the
Apostles, or is it merely the certain product of human reason working from the fact that Christ is true
God and that it is unthinkable that He should take
flesh from a source that had *ever* or *in any way* been

soiled with original sin? The question was studied
for centuries; finally there was need for an ultimate
pronouncement on the point; the Church, as the
teacher appointed by Christ, had to make that pronouncement; the Pope, as the successor of St. Peter,
commissioned to feed the whole flock of Christ with
truth and not to poison the flock with *error,* had to
make that pronouncement: and so the pronouncement was made. The whole religion of Christ was
committed to the Apostles, for they were His Church;
no *new* article of that religion has been ever pronounced *since the death of the last Apostle.* The
Church is truly Apostolic in doctrine, as she is in her
history.

No non-Catholic sect is Apostolic. Indeed, not
many representative leaders in such sects even make
the *claim* to Apostolicity. Such sects are "sects" (i. e.,
"cuts") precisely because they cut themselves off from
the Apostolic Church. Their founders were men of
comparatively recent times. The doctrines of such
sects, in so far as any clear and definite doctrines are
still preached by the sects, are not the same as those of
the Apostles. Nor are the rulers of such sects lineal
and lawful successors of the Apostles.

c) ATTRIBUTES OF THE CATHOLIC CHURCH

We have seen that the true Church of Jesus Christ
has the attributes of Authority, Infallibility, Indefectibility. The Catholic Church alone, of existing

Christian bodies, makes any real claim to the possession of these attributes. Therefore, the Catholic Church alone makes any real claim to be the true Church of Jesus Christ. Let us see whether her claim is justified:

1. *The Catholic Church claims infallibility.* Obviously, we can make no direct demonstrative proof of the justice of this claim except by calling upon truths already established, viz., the true character of the Catholic Church as evidenced by her marks. Since such demonstration would be a sort of "begging the question," we shall not attempt it. We shall merely mention that the Church makes the claim, has always made it, has made pronouncements in virtue of the justice of that claim, and has never made a pronouncement that has been in any sense self-contradictory, as she could hardly fail to do if she were a merely human institution and had set up a pretense to infallibility. Certainly the true Church of Christ would make claim to infallibility; and certainly the Catholic Church is the only Christian body that makes that claim—it is not difficult to see the conclusion to which reason points. Error simply *will* creep into the wisest plans, the most careful calculations of men, especially if the plans be of a bewildering intricacy and the calculations be extended through two thousand years of existence. And error is always suicidal; it eventually wipes itself out. A human institution, world-wide in influence, active in all times and among

all conditions of men, simply cannot endure for a thousand years unchanged—that is, if it is merely a human institution and *fallible*. If the Catholic Church *could* teach error, certainly error *would* have been taught in its turbulent history of two thousand years; and certainly error would have destroyed the Catholic Church, even if the destruction was what is called *an essential change* in doctrine or worship. Such change has not come into the Catholic Church. Great forces have been brought to bear on the Church to induce such change; innumerable heresies have tried to sway her this way or that; kings have threatened; nations have defected; persecutions have raged; yet the Catholic Church has not changed her doctrine by a hair's breadth. If the Catholic Church be not infallible, her existence is as solitary and as miraculous as the Incarnation.

No Christian body other than the Catholic Church claims infallibility. This statement is obviously true; non-Catholics will be the first to admit it. Yet Protestants, if they are true to the basic tenet of Protestantism, claim that every member of their sects is infallible—what else does the doctrine of private judgment and individual guidance by the Holy Ghost mean? But no sect, no group of sects, claims infallibility. This fact is in itself a proof of the truth of the Catholic Church and of her claim to infallibility. For consider: the true Church of Jesus Christ simply *cannot* lead men away from Jesus Christ; and if it *cannot*—as reason demands—then it is *infallible* in its teaching. Therefore, the true Church of Christ is infallible. But surely the true Church of Christ must recognize its own true character; it must claim to be what it *is*. Therefore, the true Church of Christ will *claim* infallibility because it *is* infallible and because men *need* an infallible guide to salvation. No non-Catholic body of Christians claims infallibility. Therefore, by strict reasoning, no non-Catholic body of Christians really claims to be the true Church of Jesus Christ! The Catholic Church alone *does* make that claim. Reason inexorably concludes: the Catholic Church alone has a *right* to make it, because it is the true Church of Jesus Christ.

2. *The Catholic Church claims authority.* She claims the authority committed by Christ to the Apostles when he sent them as the Father had sent Him to teach all nations and to govern all men ir. the *observance* of all that He taught. Not only does the Catholic Church *claim* this authority; she *exercises* it, and *has* exercised it for two thousand years. If her claim to authority was fallacious, millions of men, the wisest and most learned with the humblest, have been unaccountably deceived into submission to an unjust claim. Certainly Christ gave His Church authority, and just as certainly the Catholic Church is the only Christian Church exercising such authority. Therefore, either the Church of Christ has disappeared from the earth (an impossibility, for Christ, true God,

founded it for "all nations . . . all days") or the Catholic Church is the Church of Christ.

No non-Catholic group even claims a unique and common teaching and governing authority. Protestantism has no common government, and the basic Protestant doctrine, viz., private judgment of Scripture as the sole rule of faith, is especially formulated to *deny* teaching authority in the Church. The Oriental schismatics do not claim a common teaching authority or a common government, for the so-called Orthodox Greek Church is split up into about fifteen "branches," each claiming independence, and, since the separation of the schismatics from Rome, the Orientals have made no pretense to a belief in one infallible teaching authority in their "Church." Only the Catholic Church makes the claim to this unique authority, which the *true* Church surely has, and recognizes itself as having. It is not hard to see the one conclusion that reason can draw from this fact.

3. *The Catholic Church is indefectible.* We are not competent to read the future, but human wisdom confidently anticipates the continuance of what the past has demonstrated to be a persistently existent thing. The Catholic Church alone of existing Christian bodies has existed, as Christ established her, through two thousand years of continual attacks upon her doctrine, worship, and authority, through two thousand years of continual threats against her existence. Of the Catholic Church alone continuance in exist-

ence may be reasonably anticipated. No Church but the Catholic Church is Apostolic; none can therefore lay claim to indefectibility except the Catholic Church, for indefectibility presupposes Apostolicity. If the Catholic Church is not to endure intact until the end of time, where shall we find a Church of which this must be anticipated? Yet, surely, the *true* Church *will* and *must* exist intact until the end of time. Only the Catholic Church has come thus far unscathed; only she is qualified to make the remaining distance indefectibly: if she does not, none other shall. And the words of Christ must not be falsified, for He is God; He has said that His Church will endure "all days, even to the consummation of the world."

We may well close our present study by quoting the powerful words of Mr. G. K. Chesterton on the indefectibility of the Church (*The Everlasting Man,* pp. 326 f.) : " 'Heaven and earth shall pass away, but my words shall not pass away.' The civilisation of antiquity was the whole world, and men no more dreamed of its ending than of the ending of daylight. They could not imagine another order unless it were in another world. The civilisation of the world has passed away and those words have not passed away. In the long night of the Dark Ages feudalism was so familiar a thing that no man could imagine himself without a lord: and religion was so woven into that network that no man would have believed they could be torn asunder. Feudalism itself was torn to rags and rotted away in the popular life of the true Middle Ages; and the first and freshest power in that new freedom was the old religion. Feudalism had passed away, and the words did not pass away. The whole medieval order, in many ways so complete and almost cosmic a home for man, wore out gradually in its turn: and here at last it was thought that the words would die. They went forth across the radiant abyss of the Renaissance and in fifty years were using all its light and learning for new religious foundations, new apologetics, new saints. It was supposed to have been withered up at last in the dry light of the Age of Reason; it was supposed to have disappeared ultimately in the earthquake of the Age of Revolution. Science explained it away; and it was still there. History disinterred it in the past; and it appeared suddenly in the future. To-day it stands once more in our path; and even as we watch it, it grows. —If our social relations and records retain their continuity, if men really learn to apply reason to the accumulating facts of so crushing a story, it would seem that sooner or later even its enemies will learn from their incessant and interminable disappointments not to look for anything so simple as its death. They may continue to war with it, but it will be as they war with nature, as they war with the landscape, as they war with the skies. 'Heaven and earth shall pass away, but my words shall not pass away.' They will watch for it to stumble; they will watch for it to err; they will no longer watch for it to end."

In this Article we have seen that the marks and attributes of the true Church of Jesus Christ—viz., unity, holiness, catholicity, apostolicity, authority, infallibility, indefectibility—are found to be the marks and attributes of the Roman Catholic Church alone. The conclusion is inevitable: the Roman Catholic Church alone is the true Church of Jesus Christ.

Let Catholic apologists be bold to claim this truth; let them not surrender the cause of Christ, which they are to forward at all costs, by a milk-and-water philosophy of *tolerance*. Tolerance is for external conduct; it is not for the mind; the mind *cannot* tolerate error for an instant.

When the non-Catholic says, "I think all Churches equally good," let the Catholic apologist make him see that his remark is the same as, "I think error and truth equally good." When the non-Catholic says, "I think it is monstrous that you claim that you are right and all others are wrong," let the Catholic apologist answer, "Can't *you* say that of *your* religion? If you can't, why, in God's name, do you profess a religion that you are not *absolutely sure* is the true religion? You are not mentally honest if you do profess such a religion. You have no right to teach it to your children if you are not absolutely certain that it is the truth. And, of course, if you are sure it *is* the truth, then you are sure that all contradictory religions are false. My position is the only logical position; I *do* know that I am right, and in knowing it, I've *got* to know that those who believe differently are wrong. It is not a monstrous claim; it is common sense. I did not invent my religion, and then declare myself the best inventor of religions. I did not make up my belief, and then declare that others cannot make up theirs. I have accepted my faith as a gift of God, but I have incontrovertible *evidence* that it is a gift that I must take and value above all the world. *Reason* is the force and power behind my acceptance of that faith. What reason have you for accepting yours? Leave off for a moment attacking my faith, and show me the cold and inexorable force of reasoning that supports you in your attachment to your own. If you can't, then listen at least to the reasoning that I can offer for mine."

The big thing that stands in the way of the Catholic apologist is prejudice, *unconscious* prejudice for the most part. Many non-Catholics have a deeply ingrafted conviction that, whatever is true, the Catholic Church *must not* be true. Nor can such non-Catholics give any reason for their conviction. It is inbred if not inborn; and with it there exists a bitterly persistent determination not even to consider the possibility of the Catholic Church being the true Church. Chesterton truly remarks (*The Everlasting Man,* p. xvi) : "The worst judge of all [of the true Church] is the man now most ready with his judgments : the ill-educated Christian turning gradually into the ill-tempered agnostic, entangled in the end of a feud of which he never understood the beginning, blighted with a sort of hereditary boredom with he knows not what, and already weary of hearing what he has never heard." Against this prejudice the Catholic apologist must make his patient, steady, persevering claim; he must not grow weary with bearing about the burden of truth, for it is truth that he bears; he must labor in season and out of season, by life, by prayer, by example, by word wherever possible, to make the world look at the claims of truth. The world, in the apt language of its own cheap philosophy, may declare that it "can't see the Catholic Church"; but the world can't help seeing Catholics. Let Catholics be true apologists, and the world shall be made to see what now it will not see.

ARTICLE 2. THE NECESSITY OF THE CATHOLIC CHURCH

a) Meaning of *Necessity*   b) True Membership in the Catholic Church Necessary

a) MEANING OF *NECESSITY*

By the *necessity* of the Catholic Church we mean

both that it is indispensably requisite for man, and that man has an indispensable obligation of belonging to it. We have proved that Christ is God, and that Christ's Church is the Catholic Church. It follows that Christ's Church is necessary for man; it is Christ's established means for man's salvation. It follows also that man must be *required*, must be indispensably *obligated*, to acknowledge and accept the claims of the true Church—the Catholic Church—and belong to it as a true and faithful member.

b) TRUE MEMBERSHIP IN THE CATHOLIC CHURCH NECESSARY

If the Catholic Church is Christ's true Church, founded to teach and govern all men in the way to salvation, then certainly all are bound to seek and find that Church, to enter it, to live up to its requirements. Now, as we have seen, the Catholic Church is Christ's true Church, founded to teach and govern all men in the way to salvation. Therefore, all are bound to seek and find it, to enter it, to live up to its requirements.

Did Christ do a futile thing in founding and commissioning His Church? Did the all-wise God-man go to the trouble, humanly speaking, to establish a Church for all, and then not require all to belong to that Church? Is it a monstrous claim on the part of the Church to say that she is what she is? Is it a monstrous requirement made by the Church in requiring what Christ made her to require? Is it anything but the plain statement of reason, the inevitable dictum of common sense, to say that those who know the Catholic Church to be the true Church, and yet remain out of it, cannot be saved? And is it unreasonable to assert that all men are bound to show some interest and activity in finding out the true Church, and in investigating the claims of the Catholic Church to be the true Church?

The statement, *Outside the true Church there is no salvation,* means, in view of the many proofs we have offered, that there is no salvation outside the Catholic Church. Now, who are outside the Catholic Church? Those are outside the Catholic Church, and consequently outside the way of salvation, who know the Catholic Church to be the true Church, yet do not become true and faithful members of that Church. Further, those are outside the Catholic Church who refuse to interest themselves in the quest of the true Church and will not even consider the claims of the Catholic Church to be the true Church. Those who are *within* the Catholic Church are all her actual members, and also those who are not her members, but sincerely believe that the church to which they belong is the true Church. The actual members of the Catholic Church constitute the *body* of the Church; non-Catholics who are honestly convinced that their own sect is the true Church are, provided they are in the state of grace, members of the *soul* of the Catholic Church.

Membership in the true Church—whether of her body of faithful, or of her spirit or soul—are not "saved" by mere membership. Membership in the true Church, the Catholic Church, is prerequisite to salvation, but it is not all that is requisite. The members of the Catholic Church must lead lives in accordance with her teaching, they must avoid sin and keep in God's grace if they are to be saved. The actual members of the group or *body* of the faithful have here an obvious advantage over the members of the soul of the Church alone. For the actual members partake of the grace-giving Sacraments; they can have their sins definitely and unmistakably forgiven if they confess them, in sincere contrition and with determination of avoiding them for the future, to Christ's authorized minister, the priest; they can be actually united in body and soul with Jesus Christ in Holy Communion. Those outside the body of the Church, but members of its soul, have not these advantages. Therefore, let no one say that sincere non-Catholics ought not to be disturbed about their belief, but ought to be left in their sincerity as members of the soul of Christ's Church. Christ wills all men to enter His visible society for salvation, the bodily group of the faithful; He wills all to confess His faith and His Church *before men;* He wants all to have the inestimable benefits of the Sacraments and of the graces that flow to the actual members of the Church through her ministry. Let not the Catholic apologist think that he may take his ease in the comforting thought that after all many non-Catholics, many who are actual and bitter enemies of what they think the Catholic Church is, are nevertheless true members of her soul. Let him be alert for the spread and the defense of the truth. For, after all is not a Catholic a Catholic by God's gift and grace precisely that he may save his own soul and *save the souls of others* by bringing them to know and to share the great gift that is his? It is vain for a Catholic to talk of loving his fellowmen if he does not work and pray and give living good example in a tireless effort to bring his fellowmen to the knowledge of the all-necessary truth.

The religious unrest of the modern age is clearly a sign that *now* is the time for the Catholic, especially the educated Catholic, to "rise from sleep," to become an ardent apologist, to win men's attention to the Church by deep devotion to her faith and glorious loyalty to her authority, to win men's minds to the acceptance of Catholic truth by readiness and ability in showing that clear, scientific *reasoning* justifies every claim of the one, holy, catholic, Apostolic Church, the Roman Catholic Church, the true Church of Jesus Christ.

SUMMARY OF THE ARTICLE

This brief Article has indicated to us the meaning of the term *necessary* as applied to the Catholic

Church, which we have proved to be the true Church of Christ. Further, the Article has explained the meaning of the dictum: *Outside the Church there is no salvation,* and has indicated the need of ardent apologetic activity on the part of every Catholic, especially every educated Catholic.

APPENDIX

On the Bible or Holy Scripture

Here we seek to present a brief but clear and sufficient answer to the following questions:

1. What is the Bible?
2. Is the Bible a genuine and trustworthy document?
3. Can the Bible really be known as the word of God?
4. Is the Bible alone the sole and sufficient source of Revelation?

1. *What is the Bible?*

The Bible, or Holy Scripture, is that collection of writings which *the Church of Jesus Christ recognizes* as the word of God *revealed* through the writing of *inspired* men. Three things in this definition are notable: (a) Without the pronouncement of the infallible Church of Christ we should not know what writings really belonged to the Bible as the true word of God. The Bible itself does not state what books belong to it or what books are excluded from it. Only the authoritative voice of the Church, appointed to lead men unfailingly in the way of true faith and right morality, can determine this important matter. (b) The Bible contains *revealed* truth. (c) This truth is set down by men writing under divine *inspiration.* Now, inspiration is not one with revelation. A book may contain revealed truth without being an inspired book. And a man may be inspired to write that which he can learn by his natural powers without supernatural revelation. Inspiration has ever to do with *writing;* revelation has to do with the making known of truth by Almighty God. We may profitably pause upon the matter of *inspiration* to declare more fully just what it is. Inspiration involves three things: (a) God stirs the will of the writer, moving him to the work of writing; (b) God illumines the mind of the writer, either by direct revelation of what is to be written, or by guiding the writer to make the study and research that will inform him of the matter to be written; (c) God guards the actual writing, keeping the writer from making any error.

The Bible is a *collection* of inspired writings. The word *Bible* is taken from the Greek *Biblia,* which means "books." The Bible is divided into *the Old Testament* or books written before the coming of Christ, and *the New Testament* or books written after Christ's coming. These books, in detail, are the following:

The Old Testament

The Old Testament contains forty-five books. The Hebrew Bible contains thirty-nine, for it does not contain the books of Tobias, Judith, Wisdom, Ecclesiasticus, Baruch, and 1 and 2 Machabees. Protestants follow the Hebrew Bible and number thirty-nine books in the Old Testament.

The Books of the Old Testament are: the five books of Moses (called collectively *Pentateuch*), to wit: Genesis, Exodus, Leviticus, Numbers, and Deuteronomy; Josue; Judges; Ruth; four books of Kings; two books of Paralipomenon or Chronicles; two books of Esdras, of which the second is called Nehemias; Tobias; Judith; Esther; Job; Psalms; Proverbs; Ecclesiastes; the Canticle of Canticles; Wisdom; Ecclesiasticus; Isaias; Jeremias (Prophecies); Jeremias (Lamentations) with Baruch; Ezechiel; Daniel; the twelve minor prophets, viz., Osee, Joel, Amos, Abdias, Jonas, Micheas, Nahum, Habacuc, Sophonias, Aggaeus, Zacharias, Malachias; two books of the Machabees.

The New Testament

The New Testament contains twenty-seven books, as follows: the Four Gospels (according to Matthew, Mark, Luke, and John); the Acts of the Apostles; fourteen Epistles of St. Paul (one to the Romans, two to the Corinthians, one to the Galatians, one to the Ephesians, one to the Philippians, one to the Colossians, two to the Thessalonians, two to Timothy, one to Titus, one to Philemon, one to the Hebrews) ; two Epistles of St. Peter; three Epistles of St. John; the Epistle of St. James; the Epistle of St. Jude; the Apocalypse of St. John (called "Revelation" by Protestants).

Both Testaments are commonly arranged by scripture students in three groups, viz., historical, didactic, and prophetical books.

In the *Old Testament* the historical books contain the account of creation and the history of the patriarchs and of the Chosen People. The didactic books contain psalms, words of wisdom, rules of conduct and of life. The prophetical books contain prophecies, instructions, admonitions.

In the *New Testament* the historical books contain the account of Our Lord's coming, His life, death, and Resurrection; the founding of His Church and the mission of the Apostles; the coming of the Holy Ghost; the spread of Christ's Church. The historical books of the New Testament are the four Gospels and the Acts of the Apostles.—The didactic books (Epistles) contain instructions to the faithful of Christ's Church, admonitions, comments.—The prophetical book (the Apocalypse) is a series of prophetic visions relating to the future of the Church, the glory of Heaven, the end of the world.

2. *Is the Bible a Genuine and Trustworthy Document?*

For a historical document to carry authority it must have three qualities, viz., (a) it must be *authentic,* i. e., it must be really the work of the age or the writer to which it is ascribed; (b) it must be *intact,* i. e., unmutilated; it must have come down to us without essential alteration, interpolation, or excision; (c) it must be *trustworthy,* i. e., the writer must be known as one who is *well informed* in that of which he writes, and who is *truthful and sincere.* If these three qualities are found in any document, it is authoritative, and one would be unreasonable should one refuse to accept its testimony. We apply the test of these three requirements to the books of the Bible.

The Old Testament

The book of the Old Testament are *authentic*. The oldest of them were written soon after the exodus of the Israelites from Egypt. They were written by men enlightened from on high. To these facts the unanimous and constant tradition of Jews and Samaritans attests; further testimony is found in the internal structure, contents, and character of the writings themselves, as well as in the fact that Christ and the Apostles obviously knew that the Jews regarded their sacred books as authentic, and *confirmed* this belief by appealing to the Scriptures, quoting them, declaring that they must needs be fulfilled. Not all books that claimed to be sacred were accepted as authentic, but those that we have listed as parts of the Old Testament were carefully slected out from all others, guarded most religiously from earliest times, preserved and reverenced. The ancient Hebrew Bible lacked some of the books we have listed as of the Old Testament. Yet the Greek Version, in use from about 250 B. C., was the commonly accepted "canon" or "standard version" even among the Jews; and this Greek Version (called the *Septuagint*) contains all the books we have listed, i. e., 45 books.

The books of the Old Testament are *intact*. We know this from the reverence with which the sacred writings were guarded and from the fact that these books were well known and regularly read aloud in the synagogues. Interpolations, omissions, or other corruptions could not have passed undetected by a people as jealous of their scriptural treasury as the Hebrews. Besides, by order of Moses, a copy of the original was always preserved in the Ark of the Convenant, and with this, other copies were diligently compared. Again, we have the testimony of Christ, and the Apostles, who often quoted the Old Testament, referring the people to it in confirmation of truth. Christ would not have approved a corrupted Scripture, nor would such a Scripture have pointed unmistakably to His coming, His character, His office: essential alteration would have certainly mangled at least some of the many prophecies pointing to Christ (which are called *Messianic* prophecies, since they indicate the *Messias*), and Christ would surely have indicated any essential, and therefore damaging, corruption of the sacred text if such corruption had existed therein.

The books of the Old Testament are *trustworthy*. With the exception of the account of creation, the writers of the Old Testament *historical* books were in nearly every case the actual witnesses, or at least contemporaries, of the events they narrated. As for the account of creation, the long, long lives of the patriarchs safeguarded the purity of their tradition, and the jealousy guarded seclusion in which the Israelites lived guaranteed the further preservation of that tradition in its purity. Hence, the writers of these books knew what they were writing about, they were *informed*. Besides, they were sincere and truthful men, as all students of their style confess. Finally, they could not deceive, even had they wished to, for they wrote for a people who were intimately familiar, on their own part, with the existing histories and with contemporary events.—As for the didactic and prophetical books, their wondrous dignity and the elevated character of their teaching, added to the fact that their prophecies were actually fulfilled, make their trustworthiness evident.

In all reason, then, we must accept the Old Testament Scriptures as reliable.

The New Testament

The books of the New Testament are *authentic*. We know this from the fact that from the first these books were known as to authorship, and their continual use and the reverence with which they were regarded was a certain guarantee that no false notions in the matter could come to prevail. The men taught by the Apostles themselves have left writings full of quotations from the New Testament. Besides, the New Testament Scriptures were as well known to the Christians as the Old Testament to the Jews; they were *public* possessions, publicly read at times of worship, and everywhere recognized as of Apostolic origin. In themselves, the New Testament writings reflect the customs, institutions, and laws of the time to which their origin is ascribed; the language in which they are written is the language of that time; the vividness of their narrative parts shows them to have been written by actual witnesses of events known to belong to that time.

The books of the New Testament are *intact*. These books were reverently received and guarded; they were read at public worship; they were copied and distributed to different communities of Christians. Any error would have been detected as soon as it crept into a single copy. The earliest writers of Christian times quote copiously from the New Testament, and these quotations agree with one another and with the copies of the New Testament.

The books of the New Testament are *trustworthy*. All the authors of the New Testament books were either actual witnesses of what they recorded or in close touch with such witnesses. They wrote for contemporaries, very many of whom were actual witnesses of what was written, witnesses who would have been quick to detect any distortion of the facts. Besides, the moral character of the writers is known, and was ever known, to be upright, honest, holy. They proved themselves of God by miracles and prophecies; they proved their sincerity by dying for the truth of what they wrote.

Reason compels us to accept the New Testament books as reliable documents.

3. *Can the Bible really be known as the word of God?*

The Bible, as we have seen, is reliable and can be known as such. Now, this reliable Bible proposes doctrines and facts as revealed by God. Therefore, such revelation can be reliably known as the true word of God.

The wondrous unity of the Bible, considered as a single document, could not have been achieved or approximated unless one splendidly equipped and marvellously intelligent author had written the whole work. But the *human* authors of the Bible were very many. They were widely different in time, education, culture, language. No one of them, or certainly not more than a very few, could have written their part of the Bible with knowledge that it was to be joined to the other parts; no one of them could have consciously prepared his part as a logical and requisite section of the Scriptures, taken as a whole. And yet the sections fit together in such a way as to make the unity of the Bible the wonder of scholars. Therefore, the *true authorship* of the Bible is more than *human;* it is *divine.*—Suppose some sixty architects were employed to prepare plans for a building. Suppose each architect made his plans and completed them, and left them for all to see. Suppose the sixty were men of different degrees of skill, of different ideas about the kind, size, and purpose of the building designed, of different "schools" of architecture. Suppose each architect drew his plan for a complete small building. And now suppose the sixty small plans were joined together and actually found to constitute a complete, unified, and beautiful plan for a very big building! Impossible, you say. Yes, impossible except in one peculiar circumstance. This amazing result would not be impossible *if* the sixty architects were unfailingly guided by a superior power that really planned *the whole big building* and led the sixty individual architects to work, each in his own way, at a set of plans for a small building that was really only a part of the large one. In such circumstance, the superior power that guided the whole work by directing the sixty individual architects would be itself the true designer and architect of the building. So God is the true author of the Scriptures. And if this can be known, it is known that the Scripture is truly God's word.

The Bible contains statements of fact that men could not know by their unaided powers (as, for example, the order of creation, the fact of the Incarnation, etc.); it contains prophecies of things that no human or created knowing-power could foretell (as, for example, the coming of the Redeemer, at such a time, in such a place, in such a way);

it contains authentic accounts of miracles in proof of the doctrine which it (the Bible) teaches. Now miracles and prophecies and the exhibition of knowledge beyond the power of created understanding, are certain indications of a work or a word that is *of God*. Therefore, the Bible is truly the word of God.

Add to these considerations the amazing influence over minds and hearts that the Bible alone, of all books in the world, has exercised for more than thirty centuries—since the Exodus from Egypt, in fact. No human document could conceivably have been to men what the Bible has been. The conclusion to which we are literally forced is that the Bible is not a mere human document. Hence, it is a document of divine origin. And, certainly, if it is divine, it is God's true word.

4. Is the Bible alone the sole and sufficient source of Revelation?

We have a simple answer, and a sufficing one: If the Bible alone is the sole and sufficient source of Revelation, we must have God's word for it. Obviously, God's revelation cannot do for us what He means it to do, unless we know that we have it, unless we know that we have *all* the necessary revelation He has made. Now, if the Bible *alone* is God's word, God's *only* revelation of supernatural character, then the Bible will surely say so. But the Bible does not say so. Chillingworth, a Protestant divine of the 17th century said: "The Bible and the Bible alone is the religion of Protestants." If that be true, then the religion of Protestants has no authorization in the Bible; for the Bible (*sole* source of religion and rule of faith) does not *say* that it alone is sufficient. Now, there must be some authoritative rule of faith, some truly complete and sufficient source of revelation. The Bible does not measure up to this requirement. It contains, as St. Peter says in his Second Epistle (III, 16), "things hard to be understood, which the unlearned and the unstable wrest to their own destruction." Nor does the Bible contain *all* the truths revealed to men. The Bible is not in itself a sufficient interpretation of itself. There is need of an infallible living voice to give its true interpretation. It needs the infallible living voice of that Church divinely established to teach and govern all men with the very authority of Christ. The Church is established to *teach* "all things" that belong to true religion; obviously, then, it is meant to teach the meaning of Holy Scripture. Without this living and authoritative voice we should not even know what the Bible is. Without the authoritative pronouncement of the Church we should not know which of the mass of manuscripts claiming divine authorship are really the true word of God. It is the teaching of the Church that constitutes the *rule of faith*. All revelation is not in the Bible; the very revelation that the Bible is revelation, is not in the Bible; this revelation is required, else the Bible is useless as lacking authority and authenticity as God's word. We conclude perforce that the Bible is not the sole and sufficient source of Revelation.

If the Bible were the sole and sufficient source of Revelation, then the first Christians did not have this source available to them; for the New Testament was not completed, nor even commenced, until after Christ had established the true Church. We must conclude that the Bible alone cannot possibly be the sole and sufficient source of Revelation.

INDEX

If you have enjoyed this book, consider making your next selection from among the following . . .

The Facts About Luther. Msgr. P. O'Hare 13.50
Eucharistic Miracles. Joan Carroll Cruz 13.00
The Incorruptibles. Joan Carroll Cruz 12.00
Little Catechism of the Curé of Ars. St. John Vianney . . 5.50
The Curé of Ars—Patron St. of Parish Priests. O'Brien . . 4.50
The Four Last Things: Death, Judgment, Hell, Heaven . . 5.00
Pope St. Pius X. F. A. Forbes 6.00
St. Alphonsus Liguori. Frs. Miller & Aubin 13.50
Confession of a Roman Catholic. Paul Whitcomb 1.25
The Catholic Church Has the Answer. Paul Whitcomb . . . 1.25
The Sinner's Guide. Ven. Louis of Granada 11.00
True Devotion to Mary. St. Louis De Montfort 6.00
Life of St. Anthony Mary Claret. Fanchón Royer 12.00
Autobiography of St. Anthony Mary Claret 10.00
I Wait for You. Sr. Josefa Menendez 75
Words of Love. Menendez, Betrone, Mary of the Trinity . 4.50
Little Lives of the Great Saints. John O'Kane Murray . . . 16.00
Prayer—The Key to Salvation. Fr. Michael Müller 7.00
The Victories of the Martyrs. St. Alphonsus Liguori 7.50
Canons and Decrees of the Council of Trent. Schroeder . 12.00
Sermons of St. Alphonsus Liguori for Every Sunday 13.50
A Catechism of Modernism. Fr. J. B. Lemius 4.00
Alexandrina—The Agony and the Glory. Johnston 3.50
Life of Blessed Margaret of Castello. Fr. Bonniwell 5.00
The Ways of Mental Prayer. Dom Vitalis Lehodey 11.00
Fr. Paul of Moll. van Speybrouck 9.00
Communion Under Both Kinds. Michael Davies 1.50
Abortion: Yes or No? Dr. John L. Grady, M.D. 1.50
The Story of the Church. Johnson, Hannan, Dominica . . 16.50
Hell Quizzes. Radio Replies Press 1.00
Indulgence Quizzes. Radio Replies Press 1.00
Purgatory Quizzes. Radio Replies Press 1.00
Virgin and Statue Worship Quizzes. Radio Replies Press . 1.00
The Holy Eucharist. St. Alphonsus 7.50
Meditation Prayer on Mary Immaculate. Padre Pio 1.00
Little Book of the Work of Infinite Love. de la Touche . . 1.50
Textual Concordance of/Holy Scriptures. Williams. H.B. . 35.00
Douay-Rheims Bible. Leatherbound 35.00
The Way of Divine Love. Sister Josefa Menendez 16.50
The Way of Divine Love. (pocket, unabr.). Menendez . . . 7.50
Mystical City of God—Abridged. Ven. Mary of Agreda . . 18.50

At your bookdealer or direct from the publisher.

Prices guaranteed through December 31, 1993.

NOTES